MODERN COIN MANIPULATIONS

LEARN TO DO

MAGIC TRICKS WITH COINS

Sleight-of-hand as done

By T. NELSON DOWNS

WILLIAM J. HILLIAR

and others

including

A complete explanation of the world famous "Miser's Dream" coin tricks

PROFUSELY ILLUSTRATED

STEIN PUBLISHING HOUSE
CHICAGO, ILL.

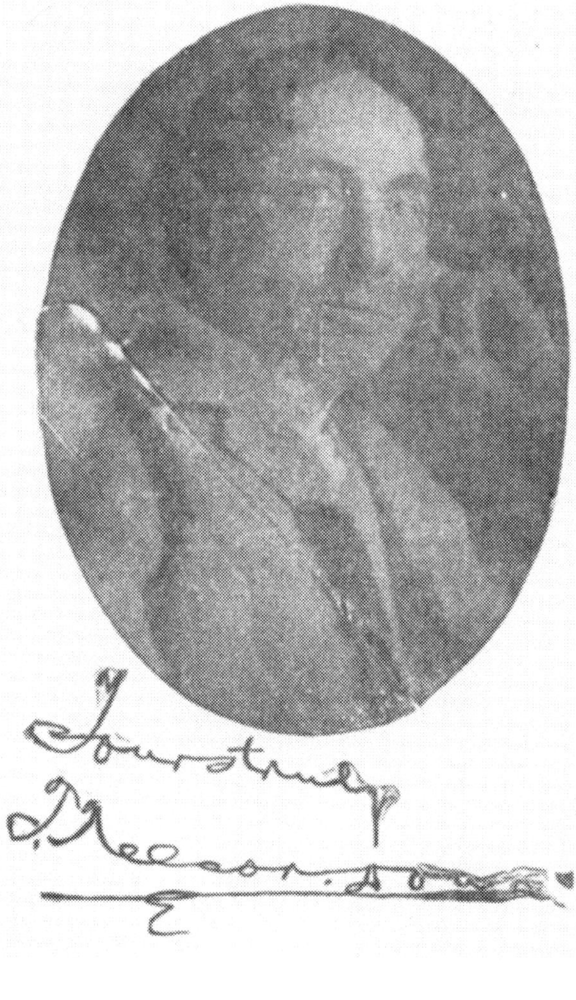
Yours truly

PREFACE

Owing to the great prejudice entertained by some performers, and others interested in magic, against books exposing conjuring secrets, the Author desires to state that this, his first, work on the subject, owes its existence primarily to the fact that people, who cannot by any stretch of imagination be called "authorities" on the art, have recently been publishing pamphlets, &c., purporting to contain a full exposure of his original Coin Creation, "The Miser's Dream." The booklets above referred to are absolutely misleading in every sense of the word, none of them even giving the elementary details with any amount of accuracy.

In the following pages the Author presents the correct methods employed by him in his celebrated act, followed by innumerable coin sleights of his recent invention, and in so doing hopes that his magical friends, professional and amateur, will consider this book an interesting addition to the already great number of works on what many consider to be the most fascinating art of the period.

THE OBEDIENT COINS

The attention of the company is directed to an empty tumbler which lies upon its side upon the table, mouth towards the audience. The glass is then placed upright, and several of the coins, which have been so magically gathered from the air, are ordered to fly into it. They not only obey the command, but they are seen to shoot into the tumbler, out of which they are then poured.

The secret is this: The coins have a small hole drilled through its bottom; likewise the table has a small hole where you stand the glass. A strong, knotted thread is passed through the coins, thence into and through the tumbler, and finally the end is carried down through the table, and out to a concealed assistant. The coins rest upon the servante of your table, directly behind the glass. A vigorous pull upon the thread will cause the pile of coins to fly visibly into the glass, and the same pull will break the thread, leaving them in a condition to be readily poured from the tumbler.

Only Nickel or Copper coins may be used.

THE DISAPPEARING COIN

The performer borrows a half-dollar, and taking it in the hand and bending the left arm ,pretends to rub the coin into the left elbow. The coin drops on the floor, but he picks it up and tries again. Again it drops, and again he picks it up, but this time with the left hand, when he takes it apparently with the right, but really, by means of the drop, leaves it in the left hand. The fingers recommence the rubbing of the elbow, as though they still held the coin; but meanwhile with left hand, which is brought by the bent position of the arm closer to the neck, drops the coin inside the performer's collar to be found at pleasure. Mean while the performer continues the rubbing, presently removing the fingers, and showing that apparently the coin has passed into his elbow, both hands being empty.

A CLEVER PASS WITH TWENTY-FIVE COINS

This is a most excellent pass, and, the author feels sure, will be appreciated. Twenty-five coins are placed in the left hand, and the right hand shown empty. The right hand now strokes the left, which is opened, the coins have disappeared, same being produced by right hand from wherever desired.

Stand with the back of left hand facing audience. The coins are apparently placed in the left hand, which closes, but in reality are stacked on the outside of fingers, being supported by the little finger of left hand. The right hand is now shown empty and passes over left, during which movement the coins can very easily be palmed off into the right hand without a sound or suspicious movement being made. The left hand is then opened and shown empty, coins being produced as fancy dictates. Five minutes' practice will suffice to show what a really brilliant move this is.

TO TELL DATE ON BORROWED COIN

This is one of the very best parlor tricks in existence. Performer, whilst blindfolded, desires spectator to hand him a half-dollar, which he (the performer) simply drops on the table, instantly naming the date on same.

To commence the trick you have a duplicate coin, the date of which you are acquainted with, palmed in the right hand, and as you take the borrowed coin between finger and thumb, exchange it for the palmed one in the act of throwing same on the table. You now state the date on the duplicate, which, upon being examined, is found to be correct.

This method is rarely detected, and produces a sensation.

Modern Coin Manipulation

CHAPTER I.

THE MISER'S DREAM.

The above original conception of the author's has, he believes, been more extensively imitated and counterfeited than any other known Magical Act. In this chapter it is proposed first to give an outline of same, and then to explain all the different "sleights" necessary for its accomplishment, which the author desires to emphatically state were all, without exception, invented by himself some sixteen years ago. He mentions this fact for the information of those who may be in doubt as to the origin of the back palm.

The stage is devoid of any kind of furniture, with the exception of an ordinary property side table, which is totally unprepared. The performer enters and asks for the loan of a hat. Upon obtaining the necessary article it is placed crown downwards on the table. Professor now turns up his sleeves to the elbows, and his hands are shown to be quite empty back and front with the fingers WIDE APART. The hat is now taken (without the slightest suspicious movement) in the left hand. The right hand next makes a grab in the air, and there are two coins, which he places in the hat. This is repeated till about 20 coins have been caught, but during the whole time the back and front and fingers of right hand are shown to be absolutely empty, and not once do they approach the body. By way of variation, a coin is sometimes passed through the side of the hat, being unmistakably heard to fall within; or a half-dollar is thrown in the air, completely vanishing, and the hat held out (a second or two afterwards) to catch the coin, which is also heard to fall into the same. A coin is placed between tips of first and fourth fingers of right hand, and pushed against bottom of hat, whereupon it instantly vanishes into the interior, making itself heard as it mingles with the other coins. The right hand now catches a dozen or 20 coins at once, dropping them all into the hat. This is continued until an enormous number of half-dollars is collected. These are turned out on the table. One is now taken in the left hand and passed completely through one and then both knees, then passed from hand to hand. Now the audience is asked to name any number, which we will say is 15, whereupon the performer proceeds to catch one at a time the half-dollars on tip of his wand, immediately passing each one invisibly into right hand, where it makes its appearance between the first finger and thumb—this being continued until the whole 15 are produced. Six coins are now vanished and both hands shown empty, when the former are produced in a fan from the back of the left hand. In conclusion, after several other sleights hereinafter described, the performer gathers up all the coins on the table—somewhere about 40—makes the pass with this huge pile, when lo! they have vanished, but are immediately reproduced in a shower from the bottom of the vest.

As the above depends chiefly on what is termed the "Continuous Front and Back Hand Palm," it is proposed to describe this in minute detail first. The object is to conceal a coin in the hand, yet at any moment showing back and front quite empty, extend the fingers and thumb is well, but immediately producing the coin when desired at the finger tips.

If the reader desires to excel in this particular sleight, he should first of all select a coin which best suits his fingers. The author always uses a half-dollar as being best adapted to the size of his hands. The smaller the coin used the more difficult to successfully carry out the trick. It is therefore advisable, perhaps, to start with a larger coin, say a dollar, and follow this up gradually with smaller coins, until you find one which exactly suits the width of your fingers.

To commence the trick the coin is placed on the front of the hand, being gripped between the tips of the first and fourth fingers (*see Fig.* 1). You now draw down the two middle fingers

Fig. 1.

until the points rest behind the coin at its lower end. If you now exert with these two fingers a slight pressure on the lower part of the coin it revolves between the first and fourth fingers (*see*

Fig. 2), and, upon the performer now extending carefully the two middle fingers, these stretch out in front of the coin (*see Fig.* 3, which represents a back view) (which is now held in same position as at first, except that it is at the back instead of the front of the hand), the coin being quite invisible and appearing to have vanished. To cover this movement, which, of course, should be executed with lightning-like rapidity, the per-

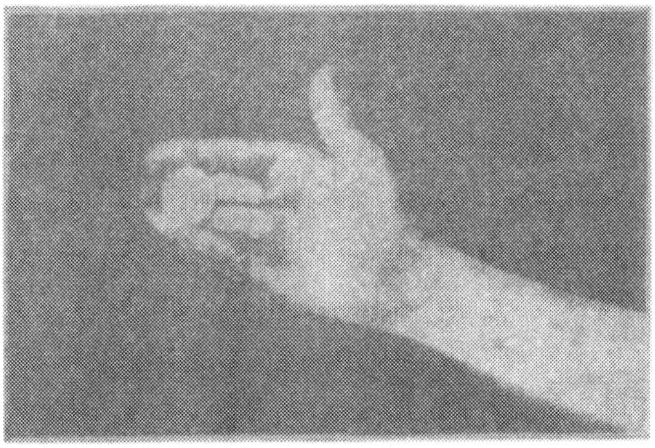

Fig. 2.

former makes a short movement with the hand as if about to throw the coin away. The slight movement facilitates the deception to a great extent. Now, to make the coin reappear, the above movements are simply reversed. This novel movement should be acquired by both hands, which should perform it with equal freedom and ease. With considerable practice this can be accomplished with more than one coin. Fig. 4 shows the author's hand with six coins back-palmed.

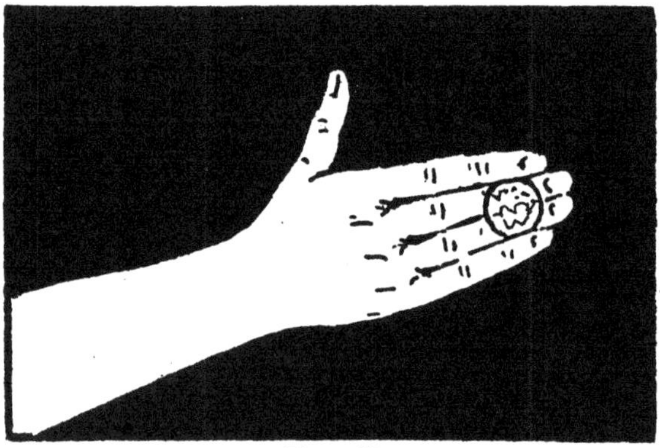

Fig. 3

The above is the original form in which the trick was invented by the author 16 years ago, but since then he has naturally made vast improvements in same, and the following is the correct manner in which he performed the "Continuous Front and Back Hand Palm" at the Palace Theater, London, in 1899, for six consecutive months. If the reader will take the trouble to compare other descriptions of this palm with the details herein given he will at once see the extent of the knowledg of the different writers who have compiled these "counterfeit" descriptions.

When the coin has been reversed to the back of the hand, as in Fig. 3, the little finger moves away from the coin, which is left gripped between the first and second fingers. The third and

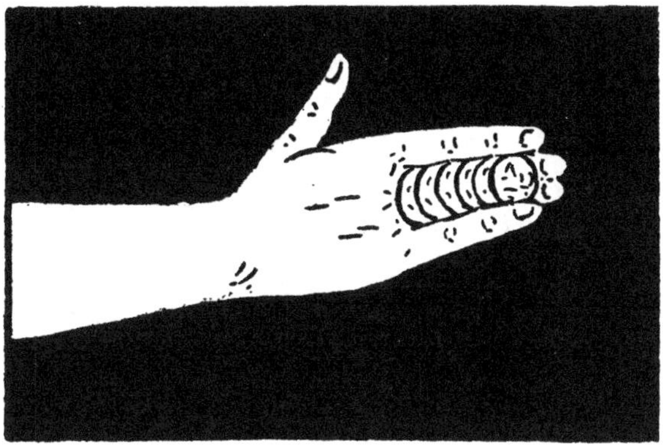

Fig. 4

fourth fingers are now spread wide apart (see Fig. 5) to show there is nothing between them. The third finger moves up at the back of the hand behind the coin, which it pulls between it and second finger, where it remains gripped as in

Fig. 6, enabling the performer to show the back of the hand, and demonstrate that there is nothing between first and second or third and fourth fingers. Now, the thumb pushes the coin through from the front of the hand to the back, still gripped between second and third fingers, enabling the front of the hand to be shown, with the first and fourth fingers extended as in *Fig.* 7.

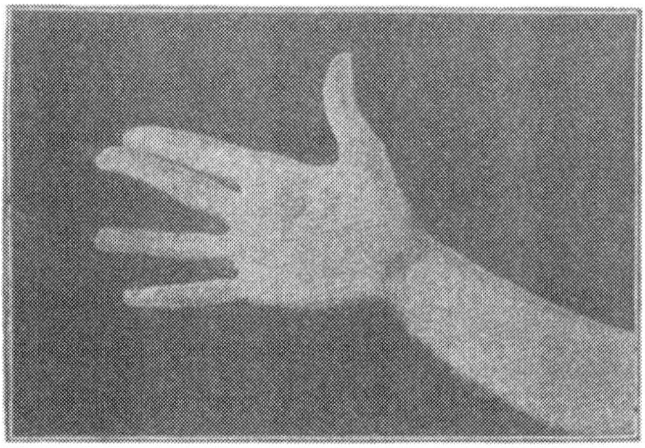

Fig. 5.

The little finger next comes up behind the hand and grips the coin in exactly the same way as the third finger did previously, enabling the first, second, and third fingers to be shown empty (*see Fig.* 8). The second finger now grasps the coin from the back, so that it is now held as before in

Fig. 7, between two middle fingers, again allowing performer to show there is nothing between first and second or third and fourth fingers. The coin is then picked up with the first finger and gripped between that and the second finger, as already seen in *Fig.* 5. Next, the fingers are bent round towards the palm, and with the assistance

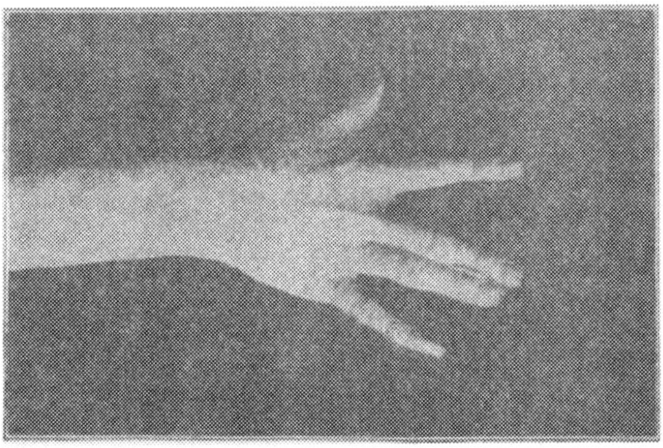

Fig. 6.

of the second and third fingers the coin is transferred to the palm of the hand (*see Fig.* 9), thereby allowing the performer to show the back of the hand with all the fingers and thumb extended (*see Fig.* 10). It is now picked up with the two middle fingers, and replaced between first and second fingers, being exactly the reverse of the previous move, enabling the front of the hand to be now shown. By next placing the third finger up behind the coin, the same can be placed at back of thumb (see Fig. 11), where it lies gripped in the fleshy part, so that the performer can now show front of hand empty, but with the fingers extended. The hand is now closed, the coin being allowed to drop in, and then opened, whereupon the coin is produced.

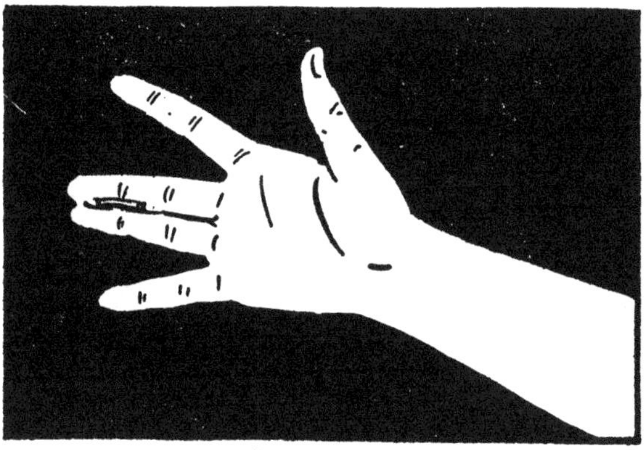

Fig. 7

The author uses all of the above passes in his entertainment, and, of course, to work the Back and Front Palm in an absolutely correct manner, a considerable amount of practice is necessary. However, to produce many brilliant effects it is only essential that the performer should be acquainted with one or two of the moves, but if the reader ever desires to become a strictly first-class Coin Manipulator he should practice, practice, and keep on practicing until all the above sleights become second nature to him, and he can then defy even expert conjurers to tell where the coin is. All the above should be done with both hands as mentioned before, thereby enabling the performer to exhibit some combina-

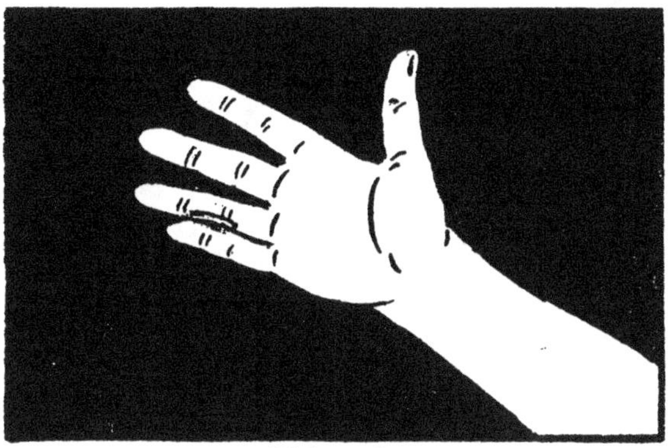

Fig. 8

tions that appear nothing short of supernatural. The author has devoted considerable space and time to the above description, but he believes it is in the best interests of the Magical Art for him to have done so, bearing in mind how professional and amateur Magicians are being deceived by productions compiled by unscrupulous parties purporting to expose his Act.

Having described the principal secret of this Act, the author will proceed to explain the Act itself and then the various additions.

Before going on the stage, the performer

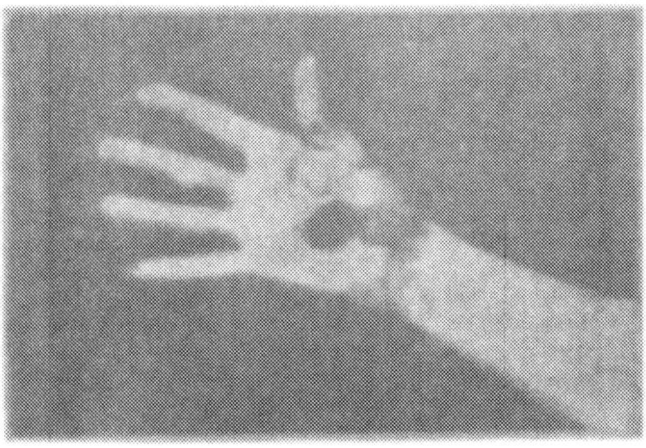

Fig. 9.

places 20 half-dollars in his right-hand waistcoat pocket, and 15 in his right-hand trousers pocket. A hat is borrowed and, while taking the same in his left hand, the coins from the waistcoat are palmed in his right, and placed like a flash of lightning under the bent-over side of the rim on the outside of the hat (*see Fig.* 12), which is placed with the same hand crown downwards on the table. Now, if the coins have been placed neatly and properly on the rim, when the hat is turned over they will remain where you put them, but this is the most delicate part of the trick, as unless you are exceedingly careful some, or all, will fall as the hat is put on the table, and, in the words of a popular song, "There would

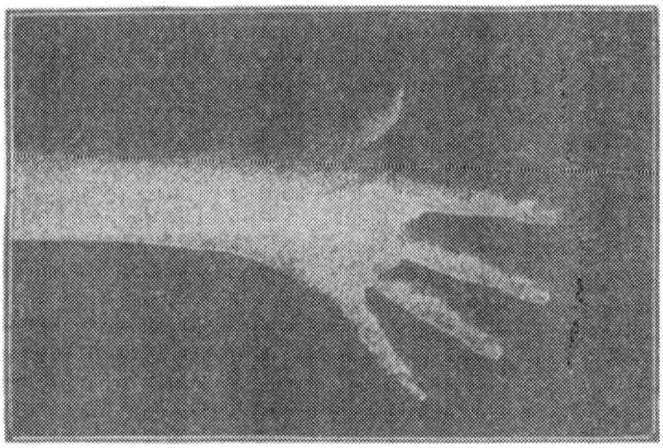

Fig. 10.

be no show that night." With practice, however, this can be accomplished. A would-be author, in "exposing" the above, not knowing how it was possible to place the coins on the rim of the hat and then turn it over, has, in his exceeding cleverness, ignored this move altogether! Yet, this is the most delicate and at the same time puzzling move of the performance. This ignorance is probably due to his "many years' experience!"

The performer now casually turns up his sleeves, and remarks, "With the permission of the ladies I will remove my cuffs, or rather turn them up to the elbows." The hat is now taken

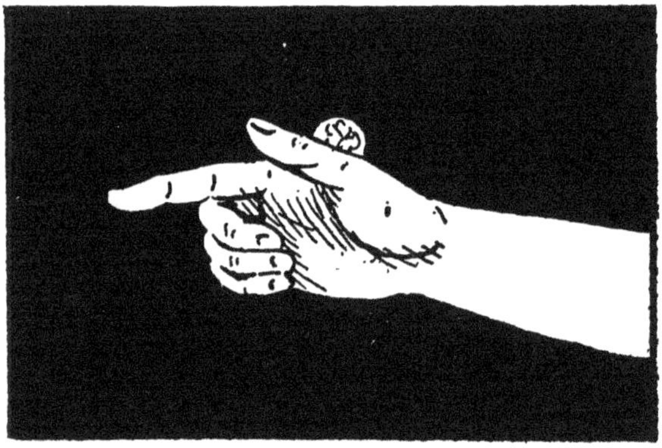

Fig. 11

up with the left hand, the fingers of which get hold of the coins under cover of the rim. The hat is next passed into the right hand to show the left empty, and the artist will find with practice it is quite easy to pass the coins with the hat from hand to hand. The hat is now taken by the edge nearest the audience, and, with right hand, turned over so that the fingers of the left hand containing the 20 coins are brought into the inside of hat (see Fig. 13), in position for the money-catching. The right hand is now shown empty, and makes a grab in the air at an imaginary coin, immediately placing it (apparently)

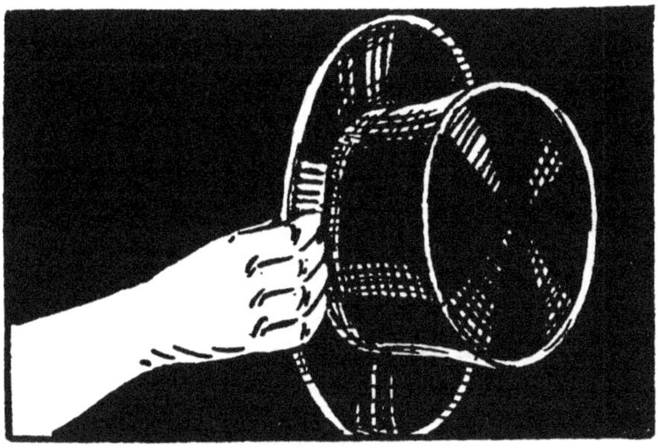

Fig. 12

in the hat, where it is heard to fall, but, in reality, it is a coin dropped from the left hand. This is repeated, and, as the hand goes to the hat to make a pretence of dropping in a coin, two coins are quickly palmed in the right hand. You look in the air for more coins, and one of those palmed is now produced at the finger tips (the mode of which is described on page —), and visibly dropped into the hat. You now produce the second one, but, instead of placing this in the hat, one is dropped from the left hand at the same moment that the right approaches the top of the hat, thereby inducing the audience to believe that the visible coin was really placed in the hat. This

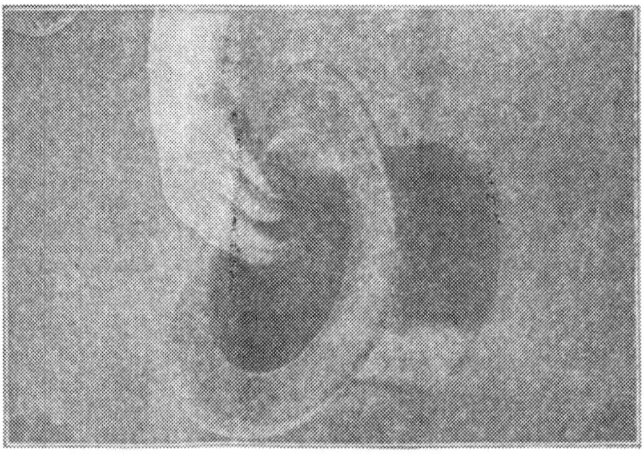

Fig. 13.

is repeated as often as desired, and, by means of the "Continuous Front and Back Hand Palm," before described, the right hand can at any time be shown apparently empty.

Additional effects are produced according to the fancy of the performer. The apparent passing of a coin through the bottom of the hat never fails to bring forth plenty of applause. This is accomplished by holding the coin in the manner depicted in *Fig.* 14. The back palm is now made (*Fig.* 15), one coin being at the same time

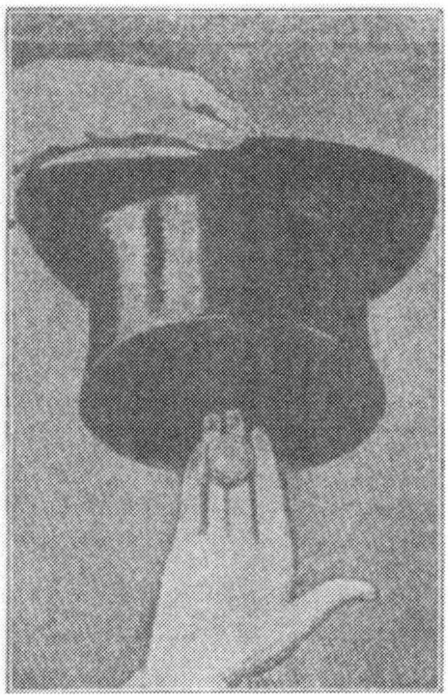

Fig. 14.

dropped from the left hand into the hat, creating the necessary "jingle," and the illusion is perfect. A similar effect can be produced by holding the coin between the tips of the first three fingers and thumb and pretending to push it through the side of the hat. What really happens is that the coin is pushed by the hat down between the fingers (the back of the hand facing

Fig. 15

the audience) which hide it, one, of course, being dropped by the left hand to create the necessary deception. It is as well to pay particular attention to these little moves, as they invariably create more furore than bigger and more difficult sleights.

A coin is now apparently thrown in the air, and caught in the hat a few seconds later. The coin is, of course, palmed in the act of throwing up the hand, and the hat is held out in the left

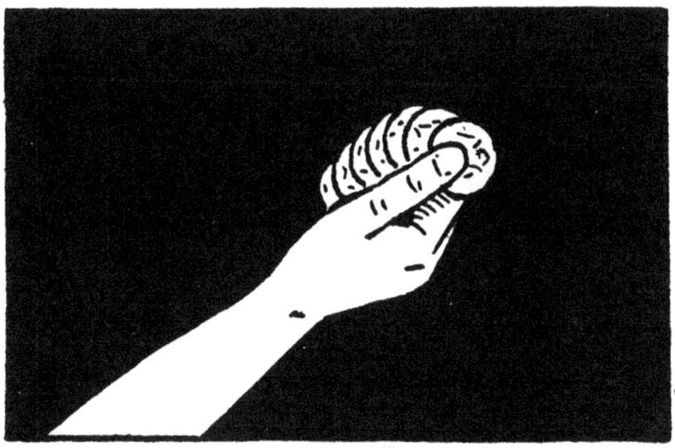

Fig. 16

hand as if waiting for the coin, which, at the right moment, is dropped from the left hand.

Wen the first load of coins is exhausted, the performer makes a bold move. He pretends to hear someone make a remark that he gets the coins from his pockets—"Which pocket?" he replies; "The left one?" and places his left hand into the pocket so as to suit the action to the word—"No, the right one?"—now placing his right hand into the pocket, which forthwith palms the 15 coins previously placed there.—"No, ladies and gentlemen, if I were to place my hands in my pockets you would all see me. Please, see that my hands do not approach the body." Meanwhile, he has got the palmed 15

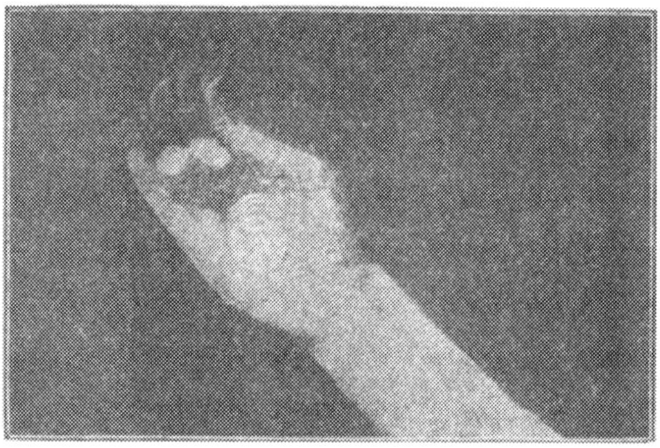

Fig. 17.

coins on to the rim of the hat as explained at the commencement of this description. The hat is then placed, if desired, on the table, crown downward, and the hands shown perfectly empty. The same process as before is now repeated.

If the above movements are executed with a

certain amount of *sang froid,* and without appearing to be in a hurry to place the hands in your pockets, not one in a thousand would guess that you were "loading"—it being so barefaced

Fig. 18.

a proceeding the audience never dream that you would be so bold as to deceive them in this decidedly simple yet effective manner.

Now, when this last lot of coins becomes exhausted, another ruse is resorted to by the performer. His right hand dives into the hat and rattles the coins to show they are real ones, at the same time letting them pour in a shower from the hand into the hat. He repeats this once or twice, and then palms, say, a dozen, which, of course, enables him to go on catching them singly (producing them at finger tips as

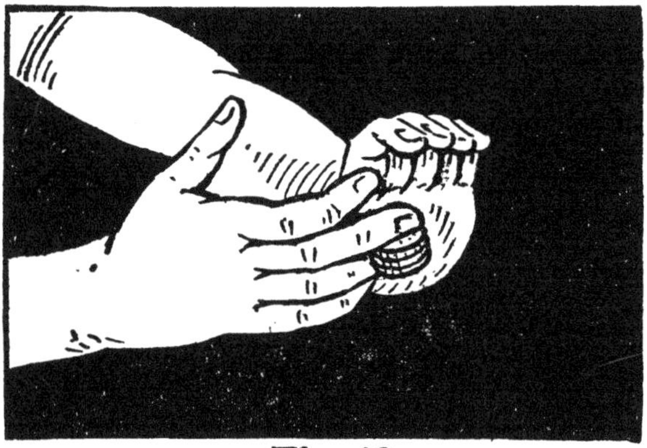

Fig. 19

described on page 28), or to make a grab in the air and produce the 12 in a fan (see Fig. 16), with the remark that "When I desire more than one at a time I make this move." The above can be repeated, if desired, but it will usually be found that 30 to 40 coins will take some time to "catch," provided the performer is not unduly quick about it. This must be avoided, and the artist must go about his business in an easy manner, without any jumps or jerks so common with unfinished performers. To practice before

Fig. 20

a looking-glass is all very well, but before your friends is better, as they are thereby enabled to give you hints as to mistakes, etc., which it is impossible for you to see yourself in a glass.

Next comes the

PRODUCTION OF ANY NUMBER OF COINS AT FINGER TIPS.

Before the hat is replaced on the table the audience is asked to name any number, which we will suppose is 15. The performer, who has in the meantime been "jingling" the coins in the hat, quickly palms the desired number, and re-

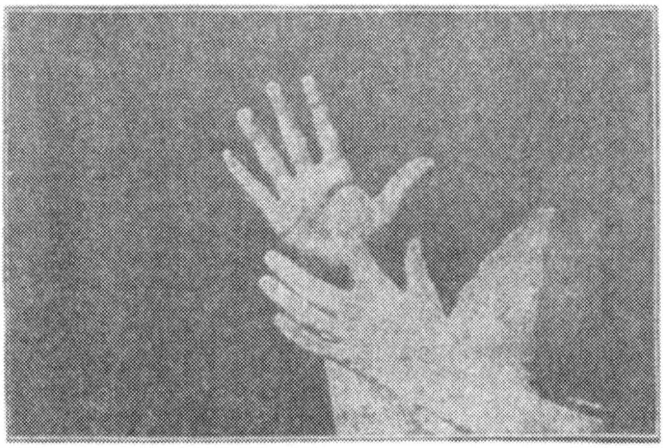

Fig. 21.

places the hat on the table (to palm the correct number instantaneously requires considerable practice, but the author is enabled through constant exercise to tell exactly how many he picks up by the feel and weight). Both hands are now shown empty by means of the "new Change-over Palm" described on page 38. The magic wand is taken in the left hand, and the coins caught on its extreme end one by one, each being then invisibly passed from the wand to the right hand finger tips. The wand used is, of course, the old "Half-dollar" Wand, but

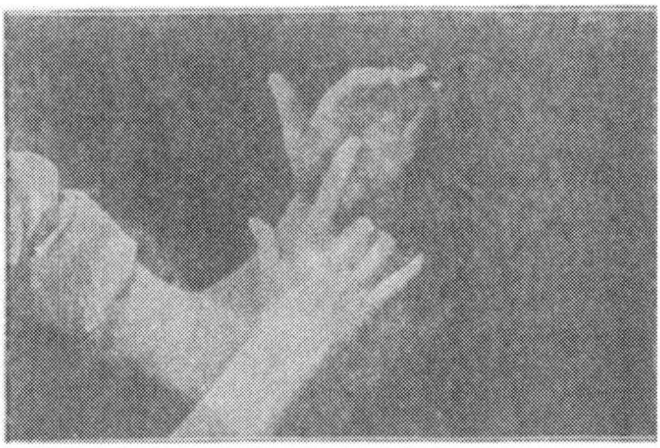

Fig. 22.

the one the author has been in the habit of using was improved by him to the extent that it works noiselessly, this being brought about by a series of minute pieces of rubber operating in the "Coin" end of the wand, which prevent the edges of the opening "clicking" together when the half-dollar is caused to appear or to vanish.

The coins are palmed in the right hand. To produce them one by one at the finger tips, the two middle fingers are bent down towards the coins as in *Fig.* 17. The third finger pushes up the bottom one (that nearest the wrist), same being immediately gripped between that finger and the second, which instantaneously places the coin between the tips of the first finger and

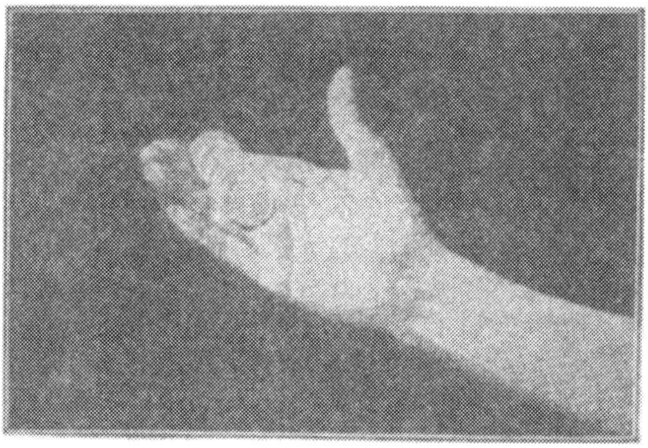

Fig. 23.

thumb, the second one being placed behind this, and so on till the whole 15 have been "produced." The left hand, of course, makes a motion of catching a coin on the wand each time and shows the coin, which is withdrawn into the wand in the act of throwing it towards the right hand.

The coins are now counted one at a time from the right hand into the hat. If, by any chance, you should have made a mistake in the number asked for, it is easy when counting them at the conclusion to "miscount" one or two.

TO PASS A COIN THROUGH THE KNEES.

To bring about the above effect a half-dollar is palmed in the right hand, and another taken between the second and third finger tips (the latter being of course visible to audience). Left hand is now shown empty, and the visible coin placed on the left fingers in readiness for the Back Palm, the left hand being placed horizontally against the right knee. The right hand now points at the coin in the left hand in a casual sort of way (in reality to show nothing between fingers or at back of hand), then shows the front of the hand (in the meantime, of course, reversing the coin to back of hand), and places it in a similar position on the opposite side of the knee to the left. *Fig.* 18 will show the correct position. The coin is now back-palmed by the left hand—at the moment of doing which the coin back-palmed in the right hand is brought to the front, the same having apparently passed completely through your knee. This can be repeated once or twice. The performer then pretends to overhear a remark, "Pass it through both knees," and replies "Through both knees? Oh, certainly; however, it's more painful," and he repeats the trick, apparently passing the coin through both knees, making, of course, not the slightest difference in the *modus operandi.*

THE ELUSIVE PASS.

The performer takes, we will say, six coins between the foremost sections of the middle and third fingers of the right hand, spreading out at the same time the other fingers, presenting to the public the back of his hand. The left hand now approaches the right as if to take away the coins (*see Fig.* 19), and, in fact, really takes them away the first time. Then, apparently overhearing a remark to the effect that they are not in the left hand, he opens it and shows the coins. Same are again taken between the tips of the second and third fingers of the right hand, and the left hand makes the motion of taking the coins, while, under cover of the fingers of the left hand, the two fingers of the right hand containing the coins are bent round the thumb of the left hand, and the coins left palmed in the right hand, the two fingers immediately returning to their original position, the left hand moving away as if it contained them (*see Fig.* 20). The above movements are made very clear in the accompanying photographs, though they may appear almost impos-

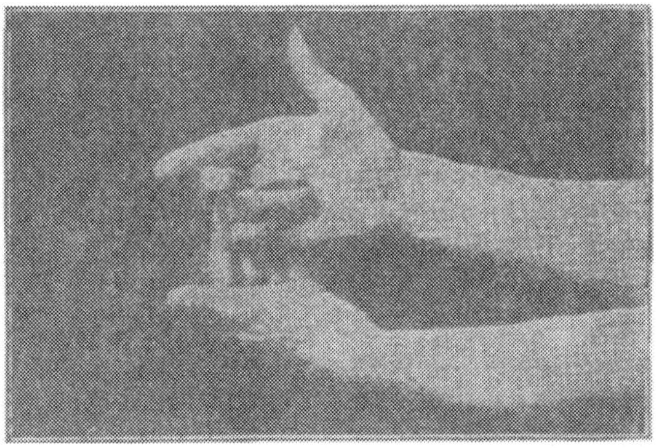

Fig. 24.

sible of execution. In the first place, the different movements should be made very slowly with, say, 2 coins; but the reader will understand that in the actual execution of this feat before an audience everything is done so quickly that it is quite impossible for a spectator to tell whether the coins are really taken in the left hand or not. Anyone who may have witnessed the author's performances will, he is sure, bear witness to this fact.

Now, upon the left hand being opened and shown empty, the right hand can also be shown empty by means of the following

NEW CHANGE-OVER PALM.

When the left hand is opened, the right hand, which contains the coins palmed, is brought face to face with the left one, and the coins transferred to the palm of the left hand, which is immediately turned round (under cover of the right) to show (apparently) that there is nothing at the back, and then the right hand can be shown empty back and front (*see Fig.* 21). The left hand is next turned round under cover of the right hand, and the coins re-palmed in right (*see Fig.* 22). This is an exceedingly difficult sleight, and requires a considerable amount of delicacy in manipulating. It is very desirable to have the coins all of the same size and thickness, otherwise one or more may slide out from the rest in the act of transference.

The coins can then be produced as fancy indicates, by catching them one at a time, or in a fan from the back of the left hand; but a suitable mode of production will readily suggest itself to a performer who has thoroughly mastered the above two passes. The author can safely state that when once proficient in both of the above the performer can do practically just as he likes with half-a-dozen coins, and he therefore considers it one of the most useful passes in existence.

DOWNS' NEW "CLICK" PASS.

As the trick about to be described relies almost entirely on the above-named new and original "pass," the author has thought it only fair to give it the above title. Once acquired it becomes a most useful and one of the most puzzling and deceptive sleights extant.

The mode of performing it is as follows:—Ten coins are borrowed and placed unmistakably in the left hand. All are satisfied that the coins are really in the left hand, they being heard to fall therein. The right hand now picks up an ordinary empty glass tumbler and the hands are held wide apart. The coins are commanded to pass *one at a time* from the closed left hand into the glass held in the right, which they proceed to do, the beautiful part of the experiment being that each coin is distinctly seen and heard to fall into the tumbler. After about, say, eight coins have passed, the performer pretends to hear someone say that there are no coins in the left hand. He immediately opens the left hand and shows the two remaining coins. The hand is closed, and the two that are left pass singly into the glass held in the right, in the same manner as their predecessors.

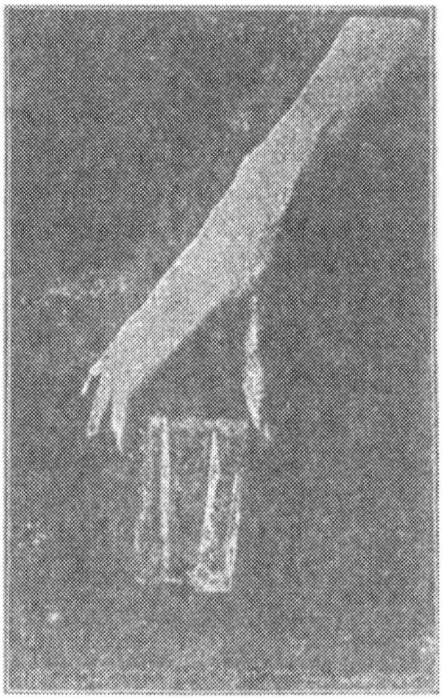

Fig. 25.

To produce the above illusion it is necessary to study carefully the accompanying photos, which explain fully the "click" pass referred to. The coins are first placed in the right hand, as in *Fig.* 23, and the hand is then quickly turned over, the coins being apparently transferred to the left hand, but in reality the third and fourth fingers of the right hand arrest their fall, *see Fig.* 24 (thereby creating a sound or

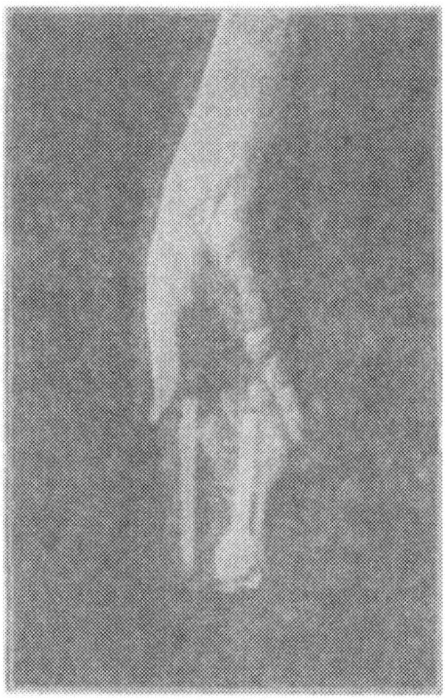

Fig. 26.

"*click*" as if the coins had fallen into left hand), and forthwith palm them in the right hand. If the foregoing be tried once or twice it will be seen what a perfect illusion it produces. Now with the right hand (containing the palmed coins) pick up the tumbler as in *Fig.* 25. By slightly relaxing the muscles of the palm of the right hand, the coins are released one at a time and fall into the glass (*see Fig.* 26). A considerable amount of practice and delicacy of manipulation is essential to ensure the coins dropping singly. The additional effect of being able to show two coins in the left hand, after eight have passed into the tumbler, is brought about by finger-palming in the left hand two dummy coins pivoted together, which admits of their being spread apart to look like two coins. These are shown, and in the act of again closing the left hand, they are reverse-palmed, the fact of their being riveted together enabling this to be accomplished with ease.

The author can confidently recommend the above trick as being one of the best with which he is acquainted, and if enough attention be paid to all the details, the performer can easily deceive expert Conjurers who are unacquainted with the *modus operandi.*

DOWNS' NEW "FAN" PASS.

This is another favorite pass invented by the author. The coins are held as in *Fig.* 27. The right fingers now allow the coins to slide down one after another with a jingle into the palm

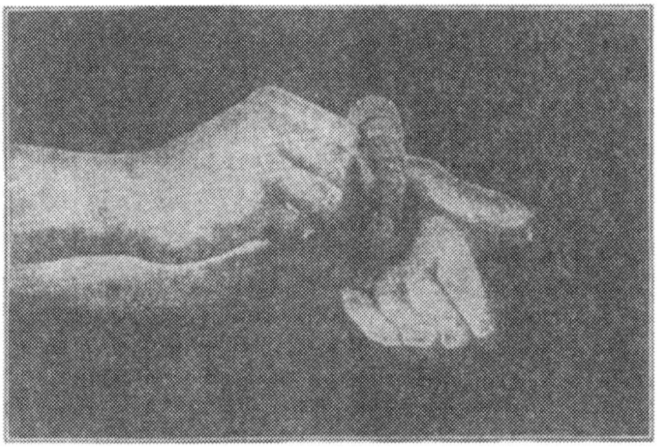

Fig. 27.

of the left hand, which forthwith closes up on the same, but just as it does so the two middle fingers of the right hand grip the coins and immediately palm them in the right hand. If this is carried out neatly, and under cover of the movement of the left hand, the spectators will be absolutely convinced that the coins still remain in the left hand.

The foregoing is a very useful method of

causing the disappearance of a number of coins after having produced them in a "fan."

THE DOWNS "EUREKA" PASS.

The author has extreme pleasure, in the following description of the pass to which he has given the above title, in taking the reader into his confidence and explaining to him fully what the writer conscientiously believes to be his most novel, puzzling and prettiest feat:—

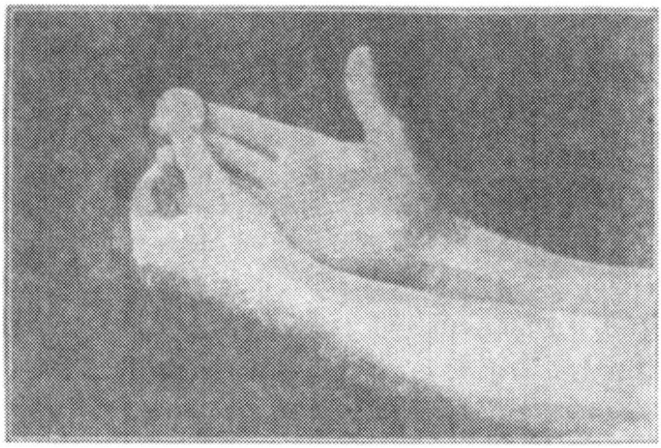

Fig. 28.

The pass is used for the vanishing of any number of coins, up to 20, one at a time.

The coins are lying on the table. One is

placed in the right hand as in *Fig.* 1 (in readiness for the back palm). This is made and both hands shown (apparently) empty. The left hand now picks up another coin by the first finger and thumb, and proceeds to place it on the right hand in the position occupied by the first (*see Fig.* 28), but in the act of doing so the middle fingers of the left hand go to the back of the

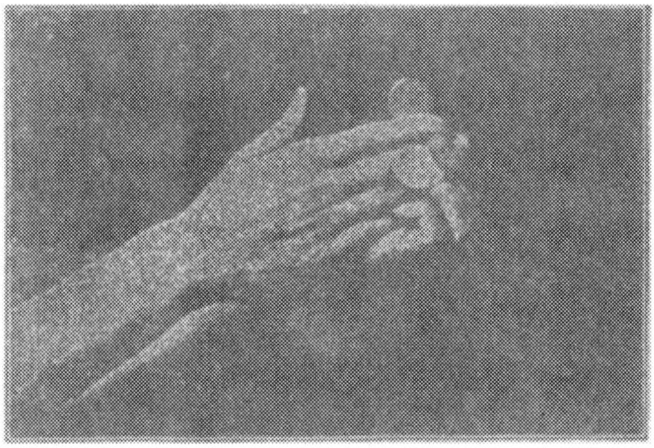

Fig. 29.

right and remove the first coin (*see Fig.* 29). The left hand now leaves the second coin on the right hand, which back-palms it, the left hand in the meantime palming coin No. 1. This is repeated until the whole of the coins are palmed in the left hand. Of course, considerable practice is necessary to palm the coins one after the other without noise, but this is not so difficult if the first coin is palmed as per *Fig.* 9, and each following one is placed under the preceding one.

THE "TURNOVER" WITH FORTY COINS.

This feat the author considers to be one of the best in his whole act, for the simple reason

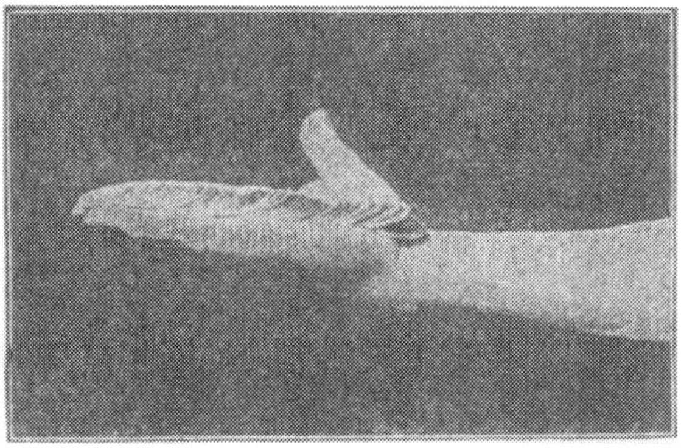

Fig. 30.

that no one has yet even attempted to duplicate it publicly. Others have tried it and have got as far as making the coins turn *one way,* but there they stop, it being next to impossible for them to make them return without the use of the other hand.

The coins are spread from the very tips of the fingers of the right hand to the wrist (*see Fig.* 30). Now, by slightly contracting the palm the whole row of coins turns completely over

Fig. 31.

in pretty fashion. *Fig.* 31 shows the coins in the act of turning. *Fig* 32 shows them turned completely over. Now by a delicate jerk with the tips of the two middle fingers the coins are made to assume their original position. The author is able to turn the coins over quite slowly and also do the reverse movement in the same manner. This makes the trick look more effective, but it is exceedingly difficult of accomplishment, though, of course, it can be done with sufficient practice. The author fears that at first sight some of the sleights mentioned in this book may appear impossible of successful execution, and he therefore begs to say that he has described nothing but what he has accomplished himself, each of the experiments herein contained being quite practical.

Fig. 32.

THREE DISTINCT METHODS OF PALMING COINS AT THE SAME TIME.

Fig. 33 represents a photo of the author's hand palming coins in three different styles: ordinary, thumb and finger-palm. It is, of course, on rare occasions found necessary to make use

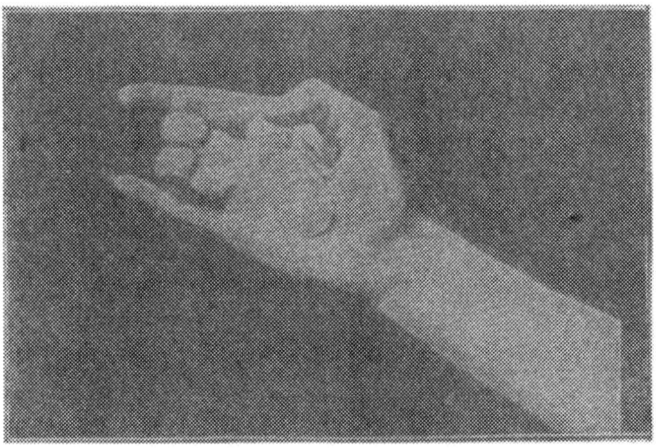

Fig. 33.

of the three at one time, but it is useful to use two of them when, for instance, the performer desires to change secretly some borrowed coins for substitutes. The latter are first of all ordinary or finger-palmed, and the borrowed ones received and thumb-palmed, the duplicates, which the audience imagine to be the borrowed ones, being simultaneously placed in full view. By means of a judicious combination of the above palms a number of excellent tricks will readily suggest themselves to the performer.

TO PALM AND MAKE THE PASS WITH FORTY COINS.

The above trick of the author's is in all seriousness described in a certain "Serio-Comic" Coin-Trick book as being "simple enough" if you do this and do that, &c. No greater mistake was ever made, dear reader, and to conclusively prove this to you the writer may tell you that innumerable imitators for the purpose of performing this feat have a wire, 2 to 2½ inches in length, soldered in a perpendicular position to the middle of a half-dollar. This lies with thirty or forty half-dollars on the table. These latter coins have in each case a small hole drilled through the center, and in gathering them up they are each threaded on the wire attached to the trick coin. It is then, of course, an exceedingly easy matter to palm them as none of the coins can slip owing to the wire.

Now to describe the correct method as employed by the author. The pile of thirty to forty coins is taken between the fingers in exactly the same manner as described in "The Elusive Pass." The right hand now makes a motion of passing the coins into the left, but in reality the two fingers holding the coins bend round and palm them in the right hand, in the position shown in *Fig.* 34, the left hand closing at the

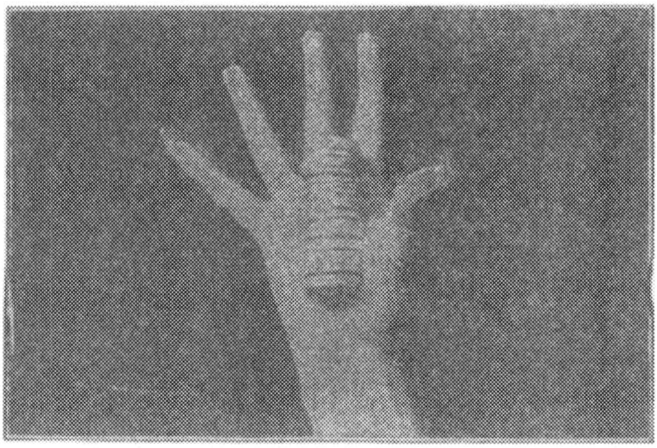

Fig. 34.

same time and the right hand keeping in an upright position pointing at the left. The left hand is now shown empty. The right hand can be brought down to hang in a natural position by slightly bending the third finger round on to the top of the coins, which keeps them from falling, and the same can be produced in any manner the performer desires.

The author's favorite method is to produce them in a shower from under the vest. This is accomplished in the following manner: As the right hand (containing the coins) lifts up the edge of the vest with the first finger and thumb, the third finger, which it will be remembered is supporting the coins, pushes them under the vest. The stomach is now expanded and the hand can almost be withdrawn, and by gradually drawing in the abdomen the coins escape a few at a time and fall into the right hand, which is waiting to receive them. In connection with the above the following line taken from *Die Zauberwelt*, of 1st June of this year, illustrates what can be attained by practice:—

"Mr. Downs has reached the highest degree of "perfection that could possibly be attained, or "ever will be attained, in this special branch of "palming coins."

CHAPTER II.

A SERIES OF ABSOLUTELY NEW AND ORIGINAL COIN VANISHES AND PASSES.

The following methods, which are numbered, are for causing the disappearance of one coin only:—

No. 1.

Encircle the thumb with a human hair loop that will reach to the centre of the back of the hand, and place a pellet of wax on the knot. Place the wax under the thumb nail. Borrow a coin and press the wax against one side. Pretend to rub it with the other hand, which drops it behind the right hand, and show empty hands. Place the hands together and bring it back to the palm. Remove the wax which you conceal under the nail again. This feat can be executed by employing the reverse palm where the coin is palmed in the fork of the thumb, the coin being dropped behind the hand instead of being palmed. The coin can then be replaced in the palm by swinging it over the hand or by using both hands. The loop can be discarded or kept on the hand.

By employing both sides of the wax two coins can be made to vanish one after the other or both at one time.

No. 2.

A spectator places a handkerchief on the table and a coin in the centre. The performer now folds the four corners over it and, on unfolding, the coin has vanished and the hands are shown empty.

This is an improvement on the old fashioned method, which the author will not underrate the intelligence of his reader by describing. A wax pellet is removed from a vest button and held between the tips of the two first fingers, and transferred to a corner of the handkerchief, which is then folded. On unfolding the handkerchief the coin comes naturally into the performer's hand. The handkerchief is nipped between the first and second fingers while the coin is taken between the thumb and the third finger tips and, under cover of the handkerchief, it is spun up the sleeve.

No. 3.

A borrowed half-dollar vanishes from the hands, and yet both sides of the hands are shown absolutely empty.

Face audience, extend right hand towards the left and pretend to pass the coin to the left, but really palm it in the right hand, which then moves backward across the bosom and shoots the coin into the vest, the hand hiding the movement.

No. 4.

In this method of causing the disappearance of a borrowed coin, a half-dollar is laid on the table in full view of everyone, yet at the word of command it instantly vanishes.

To bring about the above it is necessary to be provided with a small piece of tin painted black (as per *Fig.* 35) with a double edge. On one side of same place a dab of wax. Now palm the tin, and when taking the coin press the same on wax and place it on the table. The tin being black (the same color as table-cloth) it is not noticed. Attached to the tin is a piece of elastic running up the sleeve and, of course, at the right moment the performer releases the elastic, whereupon the coin is instantly drawn invisibly up the sleeve.

No. 5.

Pretend to pass a half-dollar into the left hand, which close, really palming it between first and second fingers of right hand, elevate left hand and bring the right to the elbow, push up the sleeve a little further, at the same time inserting the coin between it and the arm. Rub closed hand gently, open and show it is empty. Now push the sleeve again and replace the coin on the inside of the hand between the first and

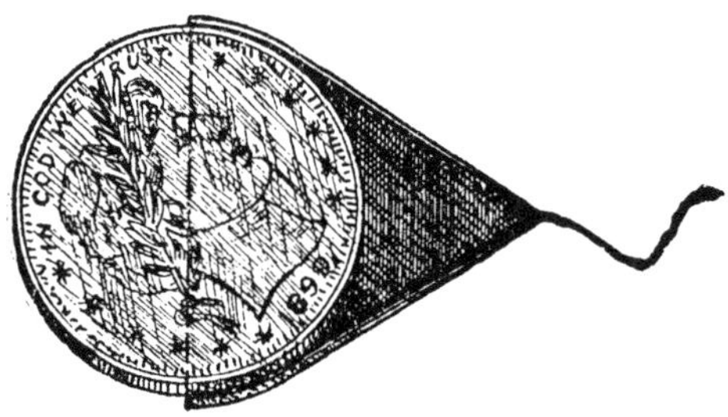

Fig. 35.

second fingers, and move the hand rapidly over the left, dropping it into that hand, which you close. Make several passes over the hand, which then open and show coin.

No. 6.

Receive a coin in the right hand, which close so that the coin lies on the bottom joints of the first two fingers, and gently press the base of the thumb against it, extend the arm to the right and insert the two last fingers of the left hand into pants pocket, and arrange the other fingers so as to form a "scoop," the thumb pressing against the side of the hand. Move the right arm around in three perpendicular circles, and during the second time let the coin fly edgewise from the right hand into the left, which allows it to drop into the pocket. The coin must pass rapidly from the right hand to the left, and always edgewise as it then exposes less surface to the action of the air, consequently its flight is more rapid. Turning the body in the direction of the arm will facilitate the move.

No. 7.

Balance a half-dollar on the middle finger of the left hand and apparently strike it with the right palm (which in reality palms it) into the left hand and at the same time closing it. This is most deceptive and quite easy of performance.

No. 8.

Performer, without the aid of any appliance, substitution, palm, pass, body, chair or table work, causes a borrowed coin to vanish from and return to the hands, the sleeves being rolled up the whole time. This is a new and unique method of vanishing a borrowed coin.

Slightly moisten the back of the left hand, receive the borrowed coin in the right hand and press it on the back of the left with the finger, where it will adhere. Open the fingers so as to show nothing is concealed between them, then place the hands together and remove the coin to palm and rub the back of the left hand with the finger tips to remove the slight indentation. Use a smooth coin for this feat, as all the sharp edges will be removed from it and thus avoid making a deep impression, which cannot be quickly removed.

No. 9.

Performer holds between his fingers a coin which instantly vanishes, both sides of the hands being shown empty. No pass, rubbers, wire, hair or appliances of any description are used.

Take the coin between the thumb and two middle fingers, and slap it on the left hand, which you close. Take up the coin and repeat. Now, as you pick it up again, throw it up the right sleeve and slap the left hand again, closing it. Show the right hand empty and push up the left sleeve. Apparently transfer the coin to the right hand and push up the right sleeve. Rub the hands together, whereupon the coin apparently vanishes.

No. 10.

The following is an extremely deceptive method of vanishing a borrowed coin:—

Hold the coin in the hand ready for the reverse palm; when this is accomplished, as you shoot the arm upward, the coin travels along the back of the hand up, or rather "down," the sleeve and both sides of the hands can be shown empty.

No. 11.

A half-dollar is shown, also both sides of the hands, to prove that no other coin is used. A borrowed handkerchief is thrown over the coin and held by a spectator. The handkerchief is held over a tumbler containing water, into which the coin is dropped by the spectator. Upon removing the handkerchief the coin has mysteriously vanished.

The coin used in this experiment, dear reader, is a "counterfeit" one, in fact, a glass disc on one side of which is a tinfoil impression of a half-dollar. This is worked off the disc under cover of the handkerchief and palmed, the disc, of course, being absolutely invisible in the water.

The following sleights are adapted for use with six or more coins, the first of which we will call:—

A NOVEL ADAPTATION OF THE "RATTLE BOX" IDEA.

Eight coins are taken in the left hand and the same is shaken to prove they are there; in fact, the coins are heard rattling till the last minute. Upon opening the hand, however, the coins have completely vanished and are produced from the air.

To prepare for this trick eight coins are placed in a piece of tubing, closed at both ends and perforated on the top and around the sides. This is then attached to a strap (see *Fig.* 36) and fastened round the wrist under the sleeve. Eight coins are borrowed and apparently passed to the left hand, which is closed (the coins being palmed in the right hand). If the left hand is now shaken the coins in the tube will, of course, rattle, and give the audience the impression they are still in that hand. The hand is now opened, shown empty, and the coins are produced from the air, as in the "Miser's Dream."

A RAPID PASS WITH SIX COINS.

Hold six half-dollars by their edges between the two middle fingers and thumb tips. Move the hand towards the left, at the same time al-

Fig. 36.

Fig 37.

lowing the coins to jump from the fingers to the palm, where you grip them.

The above may sound difficult and is, in fact, difficult when first attempting it, but with practice it is quite easy, and if properly executed it produces a brilliant effect.

DISAPPEARING PILE OF COINS.

A number of coins are shown lying on a plate, piled up, taken in the left hand where they are seen, and the hand is closed over them. A handkerchief is thrown over the hand, and when removed, the coins have disappeared.

Show a quantity of loose coins on a plate. Pile them up, and while doing so, palm a dummy "stack" in the left hand. Pretend to pass loose coins to the left hand, palming and dropping them in profonde, or in a box of bran, so that they will sink slowly and without noise. Borrow a handkerchief, show the dummy, grasp the handkerchief by the center of one side and then spread it out over the left hand, and while so doing throw the dummy into the right, the handkerchief hiding the flight. Pick up the wand, in the act of which drop the dummy on the servante, touch the handkerchief with it, place it under your arm, and draw off the handkerchief and show it, and the hands, empty; or, omit the wand business and vest dummy while advancing close to audience.

CHAPTER IV.

MISCELLANEOUS COIN TRICKS, ILLUSIONS AND COMBINATIONS.

THE EQUILIBRIUM OF SILVER.

The following trick was invented by the author as an improvement on an older trick of his in which three borrowed coins were balanced each on its milled edge on the top of a wand, which was subsequently published in one of the many books on Conjuring. The improvements on the old style will be very apparent, as in this trick the wand is entirely dispensed with, the coins being borrowed and one at a time balanced on the *extreme tip of the first finger* and then, to crown the marvel, all three are balanced *one on the top of the other on the finger tip. Fig.* 37 gives the secret of the trick; A A are two minute flesh-colored rubber bands encircling the finger and supporting a very fine flesh-colored tube through which the needle D runs, the latter being pushed up and down by the thumb. The borrowed coins are, of course, exchanged for duplicates, each of which has a hole drilled completely through from one milled edge to the other. It is therefore obvious that when a coin is placed in a perpendicular position on the finger tips and the needle pushed up into the drilled hole, it will adhere to the finger with ease. To balance the others the needle is, of course, pushed up far enough each time to enter the next coin. It is as well when endeavoring to balance the first coin to let it fall once or twice, thereby giving the impression that it is a feat of genuine dexterity.

TO PASS TWENTY COINS FROM ONE HAND TO THE OTHER.

In this trick the performer borrows, say, 20 half-dollars and holds them spread out in a fan in the left hand (palm towards audience). The right hand is now shown empty back and front, with nothing between the fingers, and is held out straight from the body. Coins now vanish from the tips of the fingers to the left, immediately reappearing in a fan between the thumb and first finger of the right hand. The same movement can be repeated as often as desired, the beauty of the whole experiment being that the palms are continually facing the audience.

The above (apparently) sensational feat is accomplished by having made *in duplicate* a stack of 20 exceedingly thin imitation coins, with a rivet running through the lot as near the edge

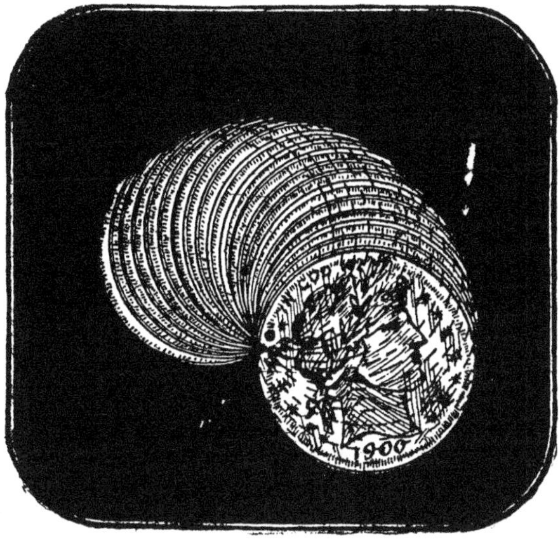

Fig. 38

as possible (*see Fig.* 38), which is soldered on to the top and bottom coin. This admits of the pile being spread out fan-wise, thereby preventing the audience from thinking you are using a dummy. This imitation "stack," being so thin and fixed together, enables the artist to make the ordinary back and reverse palm with the same. Thus he palms in the right hand one of the dummies. Borrowed coins are now taken in the right hand and apparently placed fan-wise in the left hand, but in reality he places the previously palmed dummy there, and while calling attention to his left hand the performer pockets the coins and palms the duplicate dummy, then back-palming it to show both sides of the hand empty. The rest will be obvious to the reader. The borrowed coins can be produced in the next trick, but hundreds of methods of producing coins will occur to anyone giving the matter a little attention.

QUADRUPLE COIN.

A borrowed coin is placed on an ordinary plate and immediately is increased to four.

Three coins are secretly attached to the bottom of a plate with soap. The borrowed coin is received on the plate. The hands are shown empty and the plate shifted from one hand to the other, during which a coin is removed and palmed between the fingers. The coin on the plate is now rubbed round the same and the palmed one is placed alongside it and both shown. Repeat until the coin has increased to four.

GOLD *versus* SILVER.

Two silk handkerchiefs are passed for examination, and six knots tied by spectators in each of them. The handkerchiefs are now hung from a ribbon passing between two chairs (*see Fig.* 39). Six rings and six silver coins are borrowed and placed in a pistol. The audience are now asked which they prefer, gold or silver. On receiving a reply, the performer asks which handkerchief they desire the metal to appear in. The performer now shoots at one handkerchief and then at the other, and requests a spectator to remove the handkerchiefs from the ribbon and open the knots, whereupon in each of the knots is found a ring or coin, according to which handkerchief the knot belongs to.

Two handkerchiefs are passed for examination, also two small bags, one labelled "Gold" and the other "Silver." In the "Silver" labelled bag coins are placed, in the other rings, and the strings drawn tight to close the bags. These are placed on a plate (the last person to place the coin or ring in closing the bags) held by an assistant who, on returning to the stage, substitutes two bags containing duplicate articles. He now retires and knots two duplicate handkerchiefs, which he vests, after placing

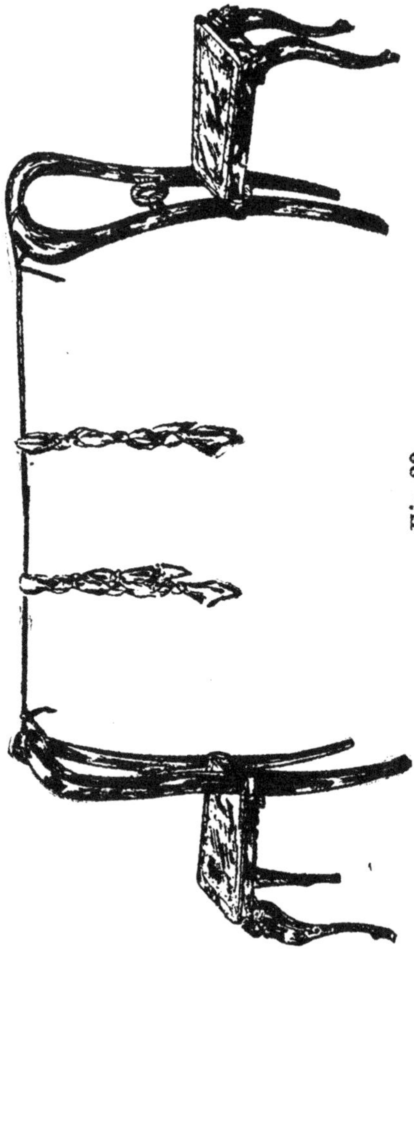

Fig. 39.

rings in the knots of one and coins in the knots of the other. The professor, in the meantime, has the original handkerchiefs knotted. These he hands to the assistant, who pockets them, and hangs the others up instead in previously arranged places. The professor now places the bags in the pistol and asks which metal the audience prefer. Then he asks in which handkerchief they desire the articles to appear. On receiving a reply he shoots a pistol at the indicated article, and then, as he does not wish his pistol—a revolver—to be encumbered with the other articles, he shoots at the other handkerchief and unties the knots, letting the articles drop on the plates and then returns them to their owners. The audience has free choice of metals, but the handkerchiefs are forced in the usual way.

N. B.—Place articles in handkerchief one at a time, and knot it so that the article is inside of the handkerchief instead of being inserted in the knot only.

THE TRANSMUTATION OF METALS.

A pile of gold and a pile of silver coins are each wrapped in a piece of paper and placed on separate plates, each then being covered with handkerchiefs. The handkerchiefs are touched with a wand and removed. On opening the parcels the silver has changed to gold and the gold to silver. Two paper tubes are now made and placed over each pile, upon removal of which the coins are found to have changed back to their original positions.

Over the silver pile place a bottomless gold dummy, and over the gold pile place a bottomless silver dummy. Take two small pieces of paper and paste the edges together, enclosing between the paper a piece of tinfoil. Wrap the gold pile in this paper and place it on the table. Wrap up the other pile in a plain sheet. Move the hand quickly over the first pile, which you pick up, and drop the other in its place. Look confused, &c., pretending not to know which is which, then tear the paper to expose tinfoil. Cover the plates with handkerchiefs after placing piles on them, touch with wand, remove the handkerchiefs and papers, and reveal the coins (dummies). After exposing the tinfoil, keep that side of parcel to the rear, so that when the handkerchiefs are removed, same will not be observed. Throw unprepared paper where audience can get it, so that they will think the second paper unprepared also. Now take two other pieces of paper and form them into tubes, and double in the tops several times so that they will retain their shape (pinning them would not be a bad idea), and cover each pile with them. Touch the piles with the wand and remove the tubes with dummies, revealing coins in their original position, drop the "fake" on servante, and hand the tubes for examination. The author considers the above an extremely neat and effective trick, and no doubt the reader will add the same to his *repertoire.*

VANISHING COINS FROM GOBLET.

Three or four coins are borrowed and dropped into a goblet, which is then covered with a borrowed handkerchief. On removing the handkerchief the coins have disappeared.

Bore a quarter-inch hole three-quarters of the way through a coin and solder a wire across the top of it. Bore eighth-inch hole through the centers of two coins and a smaller hole through a fourth coin. Tie a thread to cross bar and thread eighth-inch hole coins on, and then the smaller hole one (*see Fig.* 40), and place a wax pellet on the loose end. Drop the coins in the glass (*see Fig.* 41) and attach wax outside, and cover with handkerchief. Grasp thread through handkerchief, shake glass, and then remove them in handkerchief and drop on servante.

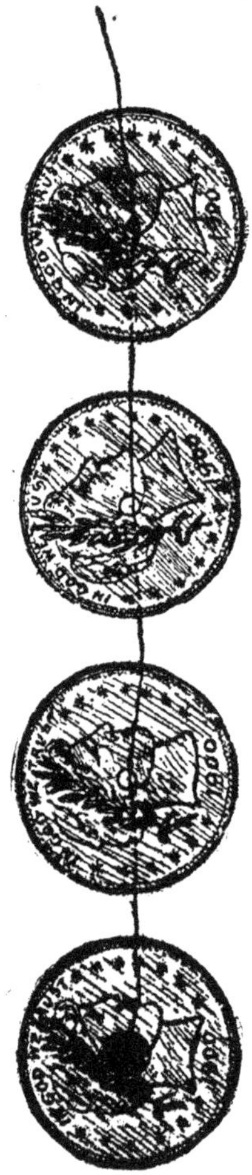

Fig. 40.

MULTIPLYING COINS.

(SLEIGHT-OF-HAND METHOD.)

Performer borrows a half-dollar, which by rubbing slightly he causes to increase to two, three, four and then five half-dollars, which can be examined. On being returned he again rubs them, when all the coins excepting the borrowed one vanish one at a time. Sleeves are rolled up

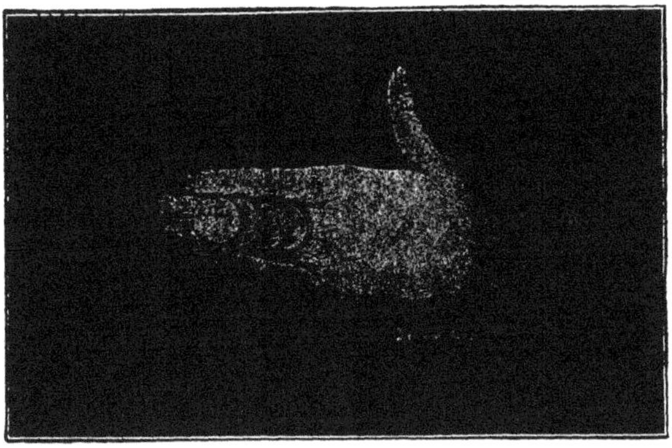

Fig. 42.

and hands shown empty before and after the trick.

Four coins are secretly palmed on the back of the hand, as illustrated in *Fig.* 42. The borrowed coin is received in the right hand, the hands are then brought together and the coins A B C D are brought to inside of hands one at a time. They are then passed for examination, and, when returned, D is palmed and then C B A slipped underneath each other part way. Borrowed coin is now returned to owner and the four coins pocketed.

NEW COIN PRODUCTION FROM BARE HANDS.

Performer turns up his sleeves and shows both hands perfectly empty back and front, fingers wide apart (no coin holders, spiders, or false palms used). He then brings his hands together for a moment, without approaching his body, and immediately produces six half-dollars.

In explaining the *modus operandi* of this experiment the author has much pleasure in acquainting his readers with an entirely original and novel method of producing the coins. Re-

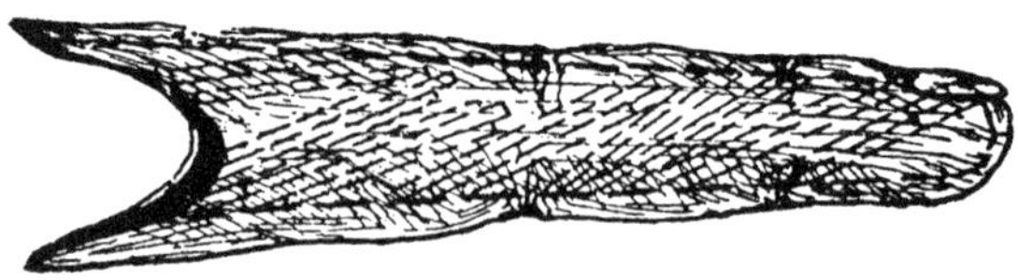

Fig. 43.

course is made to the old shell finger used for handkerchief productions, etc. This is loaded with the well-known "folding" coins (*see Fig.* 43), and placed in position on the right hand between the second and third fingers.

The hands can now, apparently, be shown quite empty, the addition of a fifth finger not being noticed if the hands are kept in motion. The hands are now brought together, the coins extracted and produced, the shell slipped back between the fingers again, or palmed, and both hands are once more shown empty.

The author has tried the above "fake" and found it practical in every way.

THE MONEY-PRODUCING CIGARETTE.

While performing the Aerial Treasury the performer fancies a cigarette, so proceeds to take an amber tube out of case, insert a borrowed cigarette (if anyone will trust him with one) in it, lights it casually and goes on catching money in the air. Suddenly a half-dollar appears at the red-hot end of the cigarette (*see Fig.* 44), at which the performer appears to be somewhat startled, but he quietly blows the coin into the hat and goes on smoking as calmly as before, the beauty of the feat being that his hands do not come near to the cigarette or holder during the whole time. This effect can be repeated as often as desired.

The above experiment, as doubtless many of my readers have conjectured, is a novel adaptation of the old half-dollar wand. The cigarette holder, although apparently an innocent piece of amber, is in reality a very neatly made money

Fig. 44.

wand, with a hole large enough to take a cigarette, but the side turned away from the audience is capable of sliding like a telescope as far as the end of the cigarette (*see Figs.* 45 and 46), and it is when in this position that the tongue moves a little stud in the mouth and

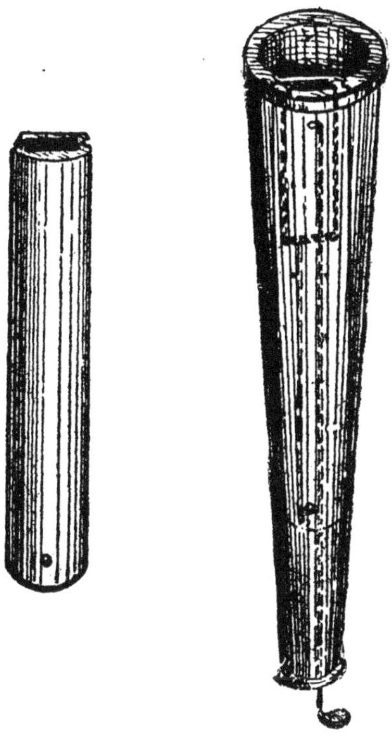

Fig. 45.
Fig. 46.

forces the coin to appear and expand apparently from the lighted end of the cigarette. By a reverse motion of the tongue the coin is made to vanish.

The above is quite a novel idea and the author trusts his readers who are on the lookout for something new—and what "real" lover of magic is not?—will appreciate it.

THE COIN OF PHOENIX.

A borrowed coin, the date of which is noted, disappears and reappears between the hands. It is then caused to adhere to the finger tip or to the wand, then it is rubbed between the hands, when it changes to a piece of paper upon which is found in writing the date of the borrowed coin. Paper is burnt, whereupon the coin instantly

Fig. 47.

reappears from the ashes and is returned to the owner. The borrowed coin is changed for a substitute and the latter handed to a spectator to examine the date, and the borrowed one pocketed. The duplicate coin is now changed for one with the edge cut so as to leave a hook as per *Fig.* 47, which enables the performer to attach it to various places. While the coin is attached to the wand, reverse-palm a small piece of paper containing the date of the coin. Bring the paper to the palm and reverse-palm coin. Show date on paper, which burn, and bring coin to palm of hand, substitute this for second coin and hand to the spectator who noted the date.

NEW MONEY-PRODUCING CARD.

Performer has a card selected from the pack, which he holds between the fingers of right hand, when suddenly a real half-dollar appears on the extreme edge of the same and then vanishes. This can be repeated *ad lib,* and would form a pretty addition to the "Miser's Dream."

Fig. 48 will explain the secret of this effect, which is really an adaptation of the old money wand. On one card is glued firmly a brass slide, B (*see Fig.* 49), the end of which opens to allow

Fig. 48.

the coin to pass out but shuts as soon as same is withdrawn (by means of springs). Another card is now glued on the top of the other one on all sides excepting at the corner where the slide opens, so that the coin can appear and disappear at will.

The card selected, which should be forced, is, of course, "changed" for the trick one, which after the trick is "re-changed" for the selected one to pass for examination.

THE MARVELOUS TRANSIT OF COINS.

Two glasses are passed on a tray for examination. The audience is requested to place a few coins in one of the glasses. Two hats and two handkerchiefs are now borrowed. A handkerchief is thrown over each glass, which is placed on top of a hat. The performer now invisibly abstracts coins from the one glass and passes them into the empty one, where they are found.

An empty glass is loaded into one of the hats. A glass containing coins is now placed in the same hat, but no, the professor alters his mind, takes it out again, and places it in the other hat. In reality he has left the glass with the coins in the first hat, and brought out the empty glass,

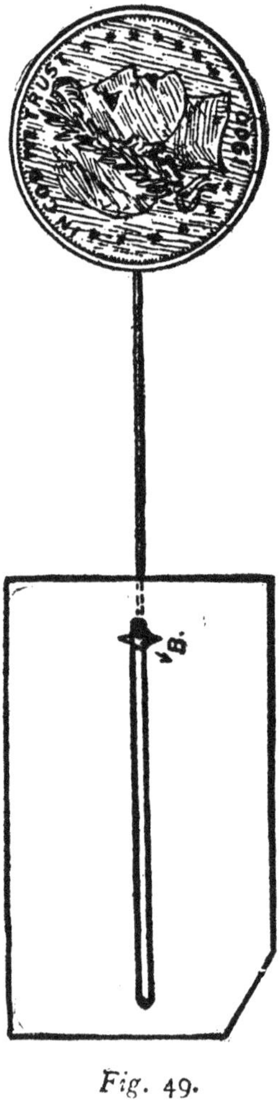

Fig. 49.

which is now in the second hat. The original empty glass is now placed in the same hat as contains the glass with coins. The latter is now picked up and removed, the empty glass being nipped with the fingers and the hat turned upside down with glass on its side. The coin glass is now placed on the top of the hat, and the other hat turned upside down and the glass placed on the top. Coins are invisibly extracted from the empty glass and shown—any palm desired can be used—coins vanish from the hand and pass into the other glass. The handkerchiefs are removed from glasses when the change is seen. Hat with empty glass under is taken to a chair, and glass dropped on servante while picking up a silk handkerchief from the top of it. One hat is now brushed and placed on the table, while the other one is brushed. A silk handkerchief is dropped on the table and the hats and borrowed handkerchiefs returned to the owners.

NOVEL APPEARING COIN.

Performer shows his hands empty and even allows them to be examined, yet upon rubbing them together a coin appears between them. This consists of a folding coin inserted in the end of wand, which is hollow, and covered with a piece of black tissue paper. After showing the hands empty, the wand is apparently pushed further under arm; in reality, however, the tube on the end of it is pushed so as to eject the coin which is palmed, the hands then being brought together and the coin produced.

THE NEW CRYSTAL TARGET.

In the following explanation of the above trick the author begs to bring before his readers what he considers to be a decided improvement on the old glass frame, and which is well worth the attention of the most fastidious performer:

Professor passes two panes of glass, six inches by twelve inches, for examination, also two rubber bands. He places the two glasses together and puts the rubber bands around them, so that they are pressed tightly together, and hangs them from a cord attached to two rods which have been previously inserted in the table top. He now borrows three or four coins, which he loads in a pistol and shoots at the glass, when instantly the coins appear between the two pieces of glass (*see Fig.* 50). The glass is removed from the cord and given to a spectator, who opens the same and removes the coins, which are returned to the owners. The glass, etc., can again be examined.

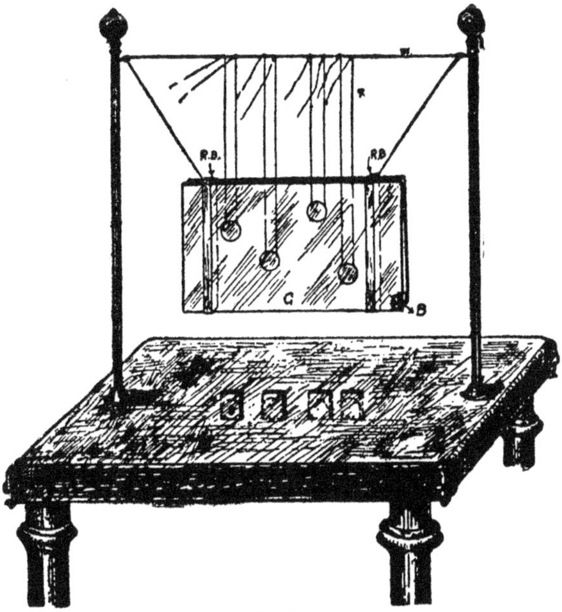

Fig. 50.

Two six-inch by twelve-inch glasses (G). Two rubber bands and a piece of brass (*see Fig.* 51) that will keep glasses apart one-half inch, japanned black. Brass is placed between glasses at B so as to keep the bottom open. Make this as small as possible. Prepare coins as per *Fig.* 52, and place in slots cut in table top. The cord passes in under the bands from the top of

Fig. 51.

one rod to the other. Double threads to keep the coins from turning are attached by wax pellets to the coins, and then passed upwards in front and over invisible wire—or to ceiling—to

Fig. 52.

assistant. After the glass has been examined in the first place, one pane is placed in front of the threads and the other behind, both are now laid down and the rubber bands put on, and whilst doing this the brass piece is put in place. The pistol is, of course, of the familiar conjuring pattern, and at the moment of firing the assistant pulls threads, causing the coins to suddenly appear between the glasses. Performer now removes glasses, the suspending cord being unhooked for the purpose, secretly getting rid of the piece of brass and brings the glasses forward, in the act of doing which the threads are drawn out, leaving the coins attached between the glasses with wax.

The above is an excellent stage illusion. The author has introduced it on several occasions, to the entire satisfaction of his audiences.

THE FLYING COINS.

Six half-dollars are deposited in a small box by the spectators and the box placed in full view on the table. Performer shows his hands empty and applies, one at a time, two circular paper discs to the flame of a candle when, as quick as a flash, they are transformed into two half-dollars, which drop from the flame. A piece of paper is shown empty, also both hands. Paper is rolled into a cone and placed in claret glass.

One of the coins now vanishes. Picking up the other it multiplies into two, one of which disappears. The coin again multiplies into two, the process being repeated until the one coin has multiplied five times and the six coins, which have in this manner been invisibly extracted from the box, vanished. On the cone being opened the coins are found therein. Same are replaced in cone, which is crushed and dropped into the glass held by spectator. Performer now causes the coins to vanish from paper and to appear in a previously examined envelope. On the envelope being opened five smaller ones are found therein and within the smallest are found the six coins.

The box containing the coins is substituted for a duplicate empty one. The best way to do this is to hold both in one hand, the empty one being underneath, the hand is now shaken and the coins heard to rattle in the uppermost box, which is immediately (apparently) placed on the table, though in reality you leave the empty one on the table. Now reverse-palm two coins in the right hand. Pick up the paper discs with the left hand and transfer one of them to the right, which applies it to the candle, and lets a coin drop. Repeat with the other disc. Multiply and vanish by reverse-palming at the back of the hand, by rubbing between the two hands, when the coin to be got rid of is palmed at the back of the hand on which they lay or by double-palming, etc., etc.

To place six duplicate coins in the zone, draw them from clip (*see "New Money Producing Candle"*) under the table top as you pick up the paper. Form it into a cone and leave the coins inside. For vanishing the coins from the cone an empty cone is crushed and palmed. Cone with coins in is taken in the same hand, crushed, and an empty one substituted and dropped into the glass.

The nest of envelopes has a tube into the smallest one through which the coins are dropped—*a la* "Ball of Worsted"—while the empty envelope is being examined. The original coins, of course, can easily be extracted from the duplicate box in your profonde* or on servante* preparatory to dropping into tube.

———

**Profonde*—A pocket contained in the tail of the performer's coat.

**Servante*—A secret padded shelf attached behind a table or chair.

The above illusion, if worked up well, with attention to all details, makes a very striking drawing room feat. The author has performed the trick with great success.

THE "DOWNS" GOBLET OF MYSTERY.

An empty tumbler is covered with a handkerchief and placed on the table, a pile of coins disappears and is found in the tumbler when the handkerchief is removed.

Fill a small-sized tumbler three parts full of

Fig. 53.

half-dollars and crush a piece of newspaper in the glass on the top of them. Palm the glass in the left hand and take an empty tumbler between the thumb and first finger (*see Fig.* 53). Throw a handkerchief over the empty tumbler, and, while arranging it, seize the coin glass and turn it upright. Drop the hands and palm the empty tumbler, and seize the other with thumb and first finger—dropping the hands to hide the exchange. Take hold of the coin tumbler through the handkerchief and place it on the table, meanwhile pocketing the empty glass. Show the pile of coins and vanish by palming. Take hold of the center of the handkerchief and paper, and remove both from the glass. Drop the paper on to servante, or else introduce the hand under the handkerchief and palm it.

THE MYSTERIOUS CLARET GLASS.

The author here presents to his reader an entirely new, original and novel "Money Catching" trick, the beauty of the feat being in the simplicity of the apparatus used. An ordinary large size claret glass, which can be freely examined, is taken in the right hand (which has previously been shown empty) and held as in *Fig.* 54.

The performer now walks round the room or

stage, and commences to catch half-dollars in the glass without the left hand approaching same. The coins are not only heard but seen to fall into the glass. The coins and glass can afterwards be handed for examination.

Grip the stem of the glass with the middle finger and palm a stack of coins on the last joint

Fig. 54.

of third finger, the middle knuckle of which rests on the top of the foot of the colored glass (*see Fig.* 55). Push one of the coins on the middle joint of the first finger and tip it up so that it falls on the thumb nail, which throws it upwards above the glass into which it is caught. Repeat until all the coins have been similarly dealt with.

The right hand can first of all be shown empty by means of the new "Change over Palm," described on the following pages:

The author recommends the above experiment as being (provided it is practiced well) a very

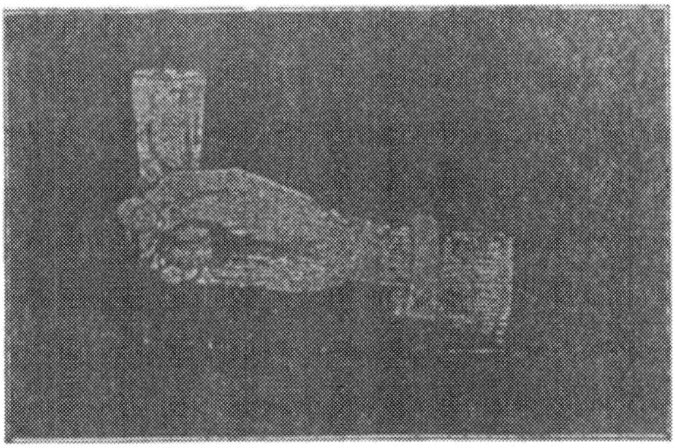

Fig. 55.

good illusion, which can be performed in a small room without anyone ever dreaming where the coins come from.

MAGNETIZED COINS.

Performer lays a number of coins on his arm so that they overlap each other. He now makes a few magnetic passes over them, when instantly they become firmly attached to each other and

Fig. 56.

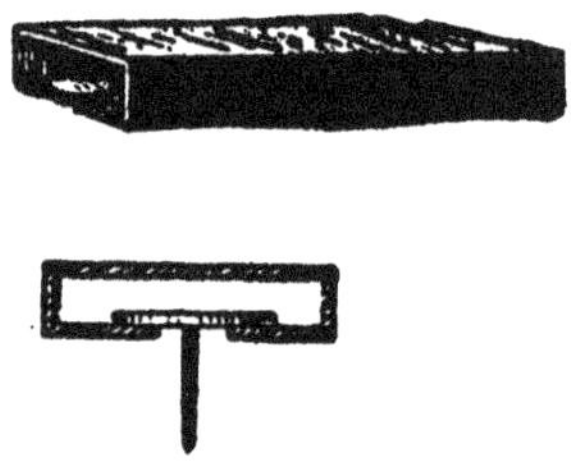

Fig. 57.

may be lifted as if made of a solid metal bar. A few more passes and the coins become as movable as before. This trick can be used in connection with any coin feat where a quantity of coins are used, and will be found extremely useful in various ways. *Figs.* Nos. 56 and 57 will explain the secret. A "T" shaped flange soldered on the tops of the coins just slides into a similar shaped groove in the bottoms of the coins.

THE DEMON GOBLET.

Performer shows a crystal goblet empty and has it examined, yet a number of coins appear in it one at a time.

Palm a number of coins in the right hand, pressing them against the wand which you hold in the same hand. Close the two middle fingers against the pile (*see Fig.* 58). Take the goblet in the left hand by the stem. Raise the end of the wand upright, at the same time pushing a coin with the thumb against the first finger. Make a downward stroke with the wand, at the same time allowing the coin to escape from the fingers into the glass, its flight being hidden by the movement of the wand. Repeat until all the palmed coins are in the goblet.

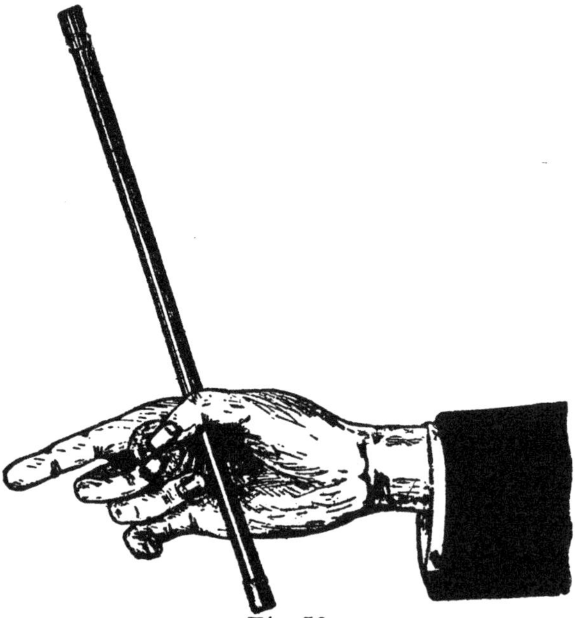

Fig. 58.

THE SILVER QUESTION.

Performer, after showing both hands empty, calls upon his banker to supply him with funds, when instantly a pile of 30 coins appears in his hand. Being for the moment like Oliver Twist, and asking for more, another pile appears, while upon making a still further request a third stack comes into view. The performer requests his banker to transfer two of the piles to his pocket. On this being done he rubs the remaining pile between his fingers and the same gradually decreases in size until it becomes a silver powder, which upon being fanned vanishes.

Figs. 59 and 60 will give the explanation of

Fig. 59.

the principal secret of this novel experiment. After the sleeves are turned up and the hands shown perfectly empty, the "load" is picked up from any convenient place with the thumb through the loop, so that it remains on the back of the hand. The hands are then brought together and the stack brought inside and the cross threads discarded. One, two, and three shown after each other, then one and two put together, palmed and pocketed. Both ends of three shown —wax on it—transferred to the opposite end and coin which keeps lower end of tube closed, and four shown while you discard three in profonde, or on servante while picking up the wand to touch pile with. Repeat with four. Now

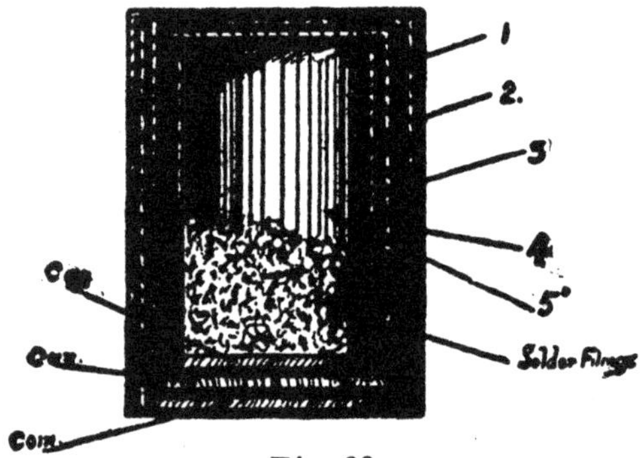

Fig. 60.

transfer coin on five to top, palm and leave filings in left hand, pick up fan, getting rid of "fake" at the same time, and fan left hand, letting the filings drop slowly on the floor.

Second Method.—Omit coins from three and four and palm the "fakes" from one to five inside of each other in right hand, and discard one after the other while picking up the fan.

Third Method.—In this way of doing the above trick you must be provided with two "fakes," one fitting over the other and the two then just fitting over a stack of real coins. Three stacks are then produced in the course of the trick, the two "dummies" vanished and the real coins can be used in another experiment.

HANDKERCHIEF AS MONEY PRODUCER.

Performer borrows a handkerchief, rolls up his sleeves, shows his hands empty both sides and strokes the handkerchief, when instantly a number of coins drop from it. This can be repeated several times.

Handkerchief is borrowed and then thrown over the back of a chair, and the sleeves rolled up. On picking up the handkerchief, a money tube made of white material, with watch spring mouth, is picked up with it. On stroking the handkerchief, the ends of springs are pressed *a la* "Shower of Sweets Bag"—and a few coins allowed to drop out. This movement is repeated until all are produced. The hand is now inserted in the handkerchief, and the tube back-palmed by means of a catgut loop fixed to it, and the handkerchief returned to the owner.

NEW MONEY-PRODUCING CANDLE.

Performer, after showing his hands empty from both sides, abstracts a number of coins from a previously examined candle for inspection.

Candle is unlighted when passed for examination. Performer, on its being returned, takes

Fig. 61.

a match from a partly opened box, as per *Fig.* 61, where it will be seen the end of the box is loaded with coins, and in the act of closing the box the coins are naturally forced out into his hand and palmed. These are then produced, apparently from the flame of the candle, and while

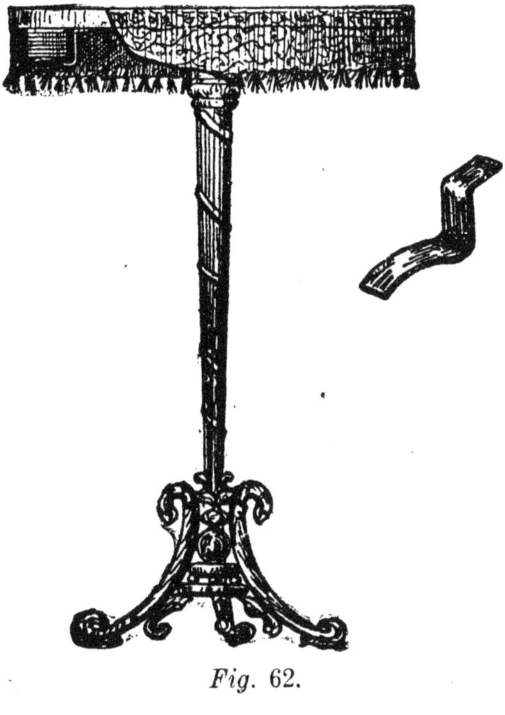

Fig. 62.

this is being done he palms another pile from the vest which are also produced. He now moves the table nearer the audience, and at the same time removes a pile concealed in a clip underneath the table top (*see Fig.* 62) which he also produces, and finally palms another pile from the vest which he likewise catches from the flame, again passing the candle for examination.

THE DEMATERIALIZATION OF THIRTY COINS.

The following experiment the author considers to be one of the prettiest in the whole range of coin conjuring. The effect is as follows:—

Twenty-five to thirty half-dollars are borrowed and marked by spectators for identity. The coins are now placed in an examined glass tube (a blown cylinder open at one end) just large enough to receive them. The latter is now corked and sealed by one of the audience, and is then held by him under cover of a handkerchief. The spectator holding the cylinder suddenly becomes aware of the fact that the same is getting lighter and lighter, and upon removing the handkerchief the coins are found to have entirely evaporated from same, and may be produced from his pocket or elsewhere at the option of the performer. The tube and cork remain intact. No confederates, etc.

To bring about the above effect you must be provided with two blown glass tubes exactly alike in appearance. One of them, however, has a minute hole in the bottom, and is filled with quicksilver and corked up tightly. The cork also has a minute hole drilled through it lengthwise. When the borrowed coins have been placed in the examined tube the same is adroitly exchanged for the duplicate (the quicksilver through the glass giving exactly the same appearance as the coins), and it is this one that is sealed by audience. Now, under cover of the handkerchief, the performer places over the bottom of the cylinder the mouth of a rubber tube, at the other end of which (in your profonde) is a bag made of the same material Now upon slightly scratching the wax from over the hole in the cork, the air rushes in and forces the quicksilver gradually out of the tube, thereby making it lighter by degrees. The rubber tube is now secretly replaced in the pocket and the cylinder handed for inspection, during which the performer has ample time to get the coins out of the original glass tube (now in pocket), palm them and reproduce them where he pleases.

The above trick affords considerable scope for comedy, especially when the tube held by spectator becomes lighter, the effect appearing to him to be that the coins are really melting. It is not at all a difficult feat to accomplish and if presented in a pleasing manner produces a beautiful effect.

COIN PASSING THROUGH A TABLE, ETC.

A coin is borrowed and the hands are shown perfectly empty otherwise. The coin now flies from one hand to the other, through a table, etc.

Palm a duplicate on the left hand two middle fingers, borrow one and pass it to left, so that it comes in front of substitute, which you push with thumb so that both come together and look like one. Now take them between the first finger and thumb so that they look like one coin and pass them from one hand to the other, exposing both palms empty. Finally, take the coin between the tips of the middle fingers and thumb. Then as you pass the "coin" to the left hand, push only the inner one into left hand, sliding the thumb over the front coin, which palm on thumb. The left hand now contains the substitute, and the right one the borrowed coin. You can now pass the coin from hand to hand, etc. Finally, again combine both and show one.

The above is a very useful sleight and the author recommends it as creating, after a little practice, a perfect illusion.

THE CRYSTAL COIN LADDER.

The trick now about to be described and known among magicians by the above title was, the author believes, invented by the celebrated prestidigitateur Robert Heller. The author performed it for some time, but, owing to its exhibition by many imitators, he has discarded it and leaves it to the other "Coin Kings" and "Queens," some of whom are now performing it. Being purely a mechanical trick, it does not, of course, require much practice, but if presented in the manner herein described it never fails to produce a good effect.

Fig. 63 shows the "Ladder," from which the reader will get a very good idea of what it is like. The "steps" in the ladder are glass slabs, the metal work all being of polished brass, with a nice gold fringe around the top, which gives

Fig. 63.

it a beautiful stage appearance. The mode in which the author presented the trick was as follows:—

Six half-dollars were borrowed, together with an ordinary silk hat. The hat was suspended at the bottom of the ladder, as in the engraving. The coins were now placed in a glass tumbler, which was covered with a handkerchief, and placed on the top of the ladder. The performer now remembers that he intended to place more than six coins in the glass, so proceeds, as in the "Miser's Dream," to catch a few in the air, which vanish from his hands and are unmistakably heard to fall into the tumbler (still on top of the ladder and covered with handkerchief). The coins in the glass are now commanded to pass *one at a time* from the top to the bottom of the ladder, which they do, falling from one glass slab to another till they reach the hat at the base of the ladder. The tumbler is now taken down, still covered with the handkerchief, which the audience remove, when the coins are seen to have vanished, and upon the hat being examined there are the coins. The six half-dollars originally borrowed are then handed back to the lender with thanks. Now for the secret:—

The top of the ladder is in reality a box containing the mechanism of the illusion. At the rear is a kind of drawer, into which six duplicate coins (or as many more as you intend using) are placed. Now upon an assistant in the wings pulling a cord, one of these coins is let through the top of the ladder on to the first glass slab, the latter being arranged so that, when a coin drops on to it, the coin immediately slides to the lower edge and then drops on to the next slab—this being repeated until the coin has reached the hat. One of the vases, apparently only placed on the ladder for ornament, is a trick one. A few coins are previously placed in the bowl of this vase and upon an assistant pulling another cord a piston rises, making these coins jump up and fall again. This latter effect is to produce the sound of the extra coins being invisibly passed into the tumbler. The glass used is first of all filled with water to prove that it is a genuine one, but in the act of throwing the water away, it is dropped on a servante behind a chair, and a duplicate one brought away, no one having the slightest suspicion that it has been changed if it is done neatly. The duplicate is devoid of any bottom. The borrowed coins are dropped into this glass, which must be held on the palm of hand in a slanting position, so that the coins drop on side of glass, thereby sounding as though the glass was quite an ordinary one. The tumbler is now covered with a borrowed handkerchief (the coins being palmed) and placed on the top of the ladder. The artist now pretends to have made a mistake in the number, and catches one at a time at the finger tips the coins he has already palmed, which vanish by means of the pass. The assistant pulls cord number two and coins are heard (apparently) to fall into the glass. Now command the coins to pass into the hat, which, of course, they do. Next remove the hat, turn it over on a plate, letting the duplicate coins fall out, but allow one or two to slip on the floor. In picking these up, mix with them the borrowed coins (which it will be remembered are still palmed) and take to the spectator who lent them. The tumbler is now taken down, the handkerchief removed, and if the former is held firm on the palm, not one in a thousand would ever dream that it was bottomless.

THE TRAVELING COIN.

For the purpose of the above trick it is necessary to obtain a very thin imitation half-dollar, through the center of which a tiny hole is bored.

Now push a pin half way through the hole and solder it in this position. Cut away the "head" end of the pin and bend the pointed end over to lie flat on the coin (*see Fig.* 64). Now glue on the back of the coin a piece of cloth the same

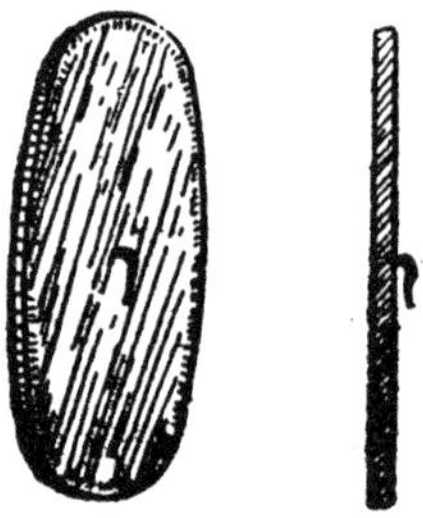

Fig. 64.

color as the coat worn by the performer, trimming it off neatly round the edges. Paint the shiny edge of the coin all round with black paint.

The coin prepared in the above manner is now placed on the table, black side up, the magic wand lying in front of it. In the act of taking up the wand the artist palms the coin. He then borrows a half-dollar from a member of the audience, takes it in his right hand (which is also concealing the faked coin). He now transfers the borrowed coin, apparently, to the left hand (in reality it is the faked one), placing the borrowed coin with the wand on table. (So that the audience cannot see the coin on the table it is dropped behind some other article over which the wand is laid.)

The performer now shows the faked coin, placing the finger over the pin when so doing to prevent it being noticed. He now lifts his right arm high, puts the coin with the left hand against the elbow of the right, fastening it here with the pin, the black side, of course, being outwards. Now he pretends to take it in his right hand (it is, of course, firmly attached to the right sleeve) and go through the same movements on the left sleeve. Then he goes through a number of imaginary passes and eventually shows both hands quite empty. The wand is now picked up, together with the borrowed coin, and the same is produced at pleasure.

The above idea admits of so many variations that the author has described it very fully. A similar idea might be very well employed in the "Miser's Dream," by having some coins similarly prepared attached to various parts of the body, which could be palmed off invisibly and eventually produced as if from the air.

THE SIXTEEN TO ONE SILVER TRICK.

In this trick the author explains his original method of producing sixteen coins, one at a time, from a borrowed one, the hands first of all being shown empty.

The method of effecting the above, which the author believes to be one of the best productions extant, is as follows:

Palm sixteen coins in the right hand in the same manner as in *Fig.* 34. Now receive the borrowed coin in the left hand and proceed by means of the new "change over palm" described on page 69 to show both hands otherwise empty. After the audience is convinced that nothing is concealed in your hands, take the borrowed half-dollar as in *Fig.* 65. The left hand now slowly passes over the right, under cover of which pick up a coin from the palmed lot, with the aid of the second and third fingers of right hand, and place it behind the borrowed one, the effect to the audience being that the left hand has simply passed over the right. To add additional effect the left hand can again pass over the right and then with the tips of the first finger and thumb remove the hindermost coin, it appearing to the audience that same was actually pulled out of the borrowed coin. This is, of course, repeated with the remainder.

A quarter of an hour's practice, after the "picking up" movement has been acquired, will be sufficient to prove what an effective "production" the foregoing is.

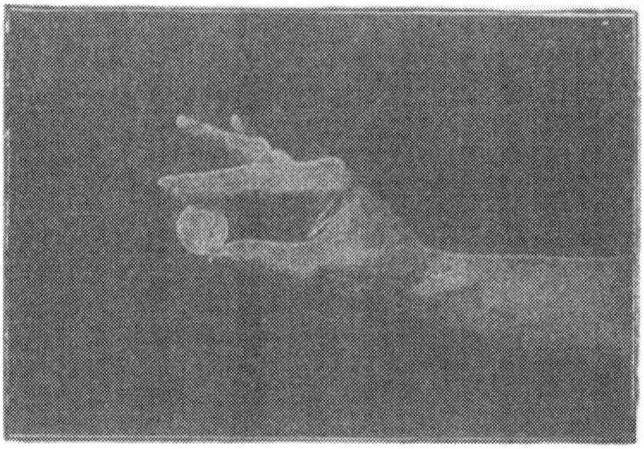

Fig. 65.

THE FUSIBLE COINS.

The performer takes one or more coins between his fingers, when they melt and the molten metal flows out of his hands. When it has again solidified, he takes it into his hand and converts it into metallic vapor, which is seen to issue from between the fingers. Then he catches with his empty hands in the smoke clouds and produces the coins in their original shape.

To perform this trick it is necessary to be provided with:

(1) A little holder (*see Fig.* 66) about the

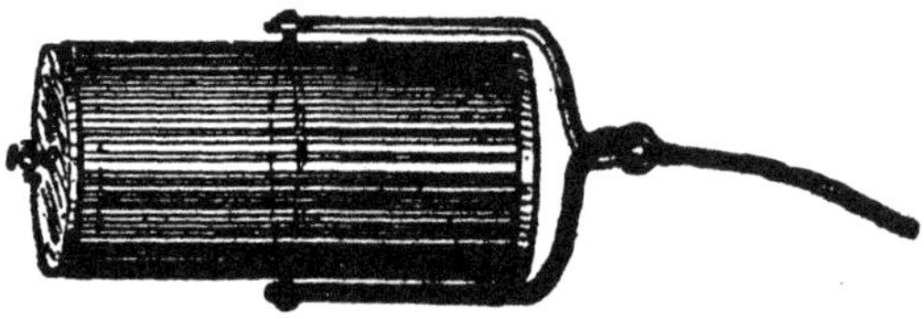

Fig. 66.

size and shape of the well known pull cup used for causing the change and disappearance of a handkerchief. This holder, which is also attached by means of a rubber cord to the back of the vest, is divided in the middle, opening at either end. One end is provided with a rubber cork in which a tube is inserted, provided on the outside with a little tap. This small holder is filled with mercury. The other end is first of all rinsed out with hydrochloric acid and a little cap fitting on same is similarly prepared with liquid ammonia. The cap is now placed on. The two chemicals combining form a vapor.

(2) A small metal basin (*see Fig.* 67) really consisting of two parts, the outside one being

Fig. 67.

deeper than the other, which has a minute hole in the bottom, so that a vacant space is created between the two. (*See Fig.* 68, which gives a section of same.)

Fig. 68.

The performer commences the trick by passing the coins apparently into the left hand (really palming them in the right) which passes backwards and forwards over a lighted candle on the table, the right hand meanwhile getting rid of coins noiselessly on servante. Under cover of the movements of the left hand over the candle, the right hand obtains possession of the holder from the right sleeve. Performer explains that the coins are by this time melted. Hands are now placed together, taking care that the presence of the "fake" is not detected. The little tap is opened and the mercury allowed to escape through the fingers into a glass beneath. The tap is now closed and the "pull" allowed to fly back up the sleeve. Performer now exhibits the mercury in the glass, stating that it is the silver of the molten coins. He now says that he will convert it into its original rough solid state and for this purpose pours it into the little bowl before described, which is placed for good effect, if possible, on a piece of ice. If no ice is available make use of a fan. The mercury of course at once disappears through the tiny hole in false bottom in the bowl. This done, the performer, under pretense of showing how the process is being accomplished, grasps the bowl, at the same time secretly inserting a lump of Wood's metal, which melts at about 68 degrees C. This might be introduced before the mercury is poured in, the precise method employed, however, being immaterial so long as it is inserted indetectably. After a time he turns out the same on to the table.

"You seem inclined to think that I am merely telling you a pretty story, ladies and gentlemen. Please look for yourselves. Here you can see the erstwhile molten metal is quite solid" (he taps the table with the lump, showing in the meantime the empty bowl). "If you think it not the same you have just seen in its liquid condition I shall be only too pleased to show you that you are mistaken by performing the experiment in another manner. Now watch me closely. I place the lump into glass filled with water and put it on a tripod, over which I place a wire gauze. Now I warm the water by the aid of this spirit lamp. A short period of time will be adequate to melt the silver before your gaze in the transparent glass." (He now pours out carefully the hot water—letting the liquid metal out on to a sheet of paper; the paper is not charred by it.) "This peculiar change in the properties of the silver, which has usually rather a high melting point, has been brought about by my magic touch. Meanwhile, as you all can see, the metal has again become solid matter. The paper is absolutely undamaged. I shall now proceed by taking this solid lump in the left hand (really palming it in the right) and hold it over the candle in this manner." (The right hand meanwhile gets down "pull," turns it round, so as to get the smoke end facing the front, the hands are now brought together, smoke cap removed and smoke allowed to escape through fingers, "pull" released and allowed to go back into sleeve.) "As you can see, ladies and gentlemen, the transformation is now an accomplished fact. The metal, having first of all changed into a liquid state, has now been turned into vapor. The coins would be lost forever if I waited until the fumes disperse, so all I have to do is to catch at the vapor and here we have a coin, here another" (and so on, until all have been produced). "Here we find the coins have now returned to their original condition, none the worse for their mysterious travels."

The mode of producing the coins is as follows:

The left hand (left side facing audience) makes a grab in the air, the right hand at the same moment palming from the pocket the correct number of coins used. Now make a half turn to the left, the right hand grabs at the smoke, the two hands come together and pretend to knead the vapor into its proper shape and then show one coin. This is repeated until all have been "caught."

CHAPTER V.

MECHANICAL DEVICES FOR PERFOMING "THE MISER'S DREAM."

In this chapter it is proposed to describe all the latest devices invented to imitate the author's methods of palming with coins. First of all will be explained a number of mechanical coins each being so constructed that the "Continuous Back and Front Palm" can be performed with comparative ease.

The author intends, in the first place, to describe what he considers to be one of the best coins of the above description, inasmuch as the performer can casually throw same in the air or from hand to hand, even at close quarters, and defy detection. *Fig.* 69 explains the manner in which the coin is prepared. A wire loop, large enough to easily encircle the middle finger is attached to a coin by means of a minute hinge. This latter arrangement admits of the loop being laid flat on the coin (*Fig.* 70), in which position it is absolutely invisible even at close quarters. The coin is now placed on the extended fingers of right hand, the loop being slipped over the second finger. It will be found that the coin can now be swung invisibly to the back of the hand, and again brought to the front with great ease.

Fig. 69.

The author specially recommends anyone not inclined to devote sufficient time to practicing the sleight-of-hand method to purchase one of these coins, as the back palm can then be executed in a few minutes.

The next coin to be described, coming within

Fig. 70.

the above category, is that depicted in *Fig.* 71. Two thin coins are first of all brazed together with a spindle, running freely through same (shown by the dotted line in the illustration). Attached by a piece of wire to this spindle is a flesh colored arrangement which, in reality, con-

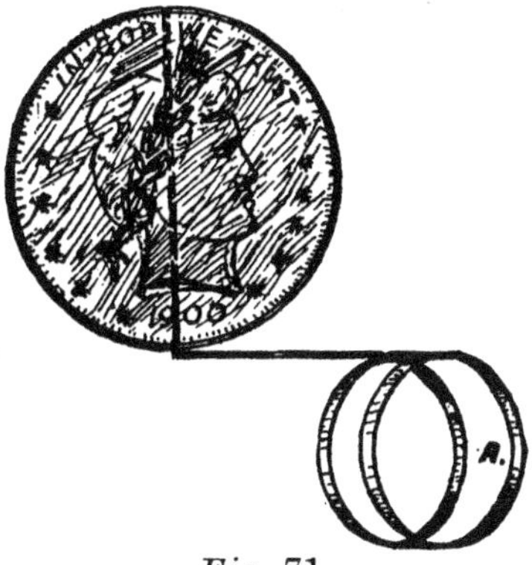

Fig. 71.

sists of two rings of just sufficient size to fit on the first finger. The finger is placed through the rings or loops in such a manner that the coin lies almost at the tips of the two middle fingers, which, if brought down under the coin, in a similar manner to that described in *Fig.* 2, cause the coin to revolve and disappear to the back of the hand. To bring it to the front again the movement is simply reversed.

Another single coin "fake" for performing the Back and Front Palm is that depicted in *Fig.* 72: A A are two hooks for clipping the knuckle ends of the first and fourth fingers, at-

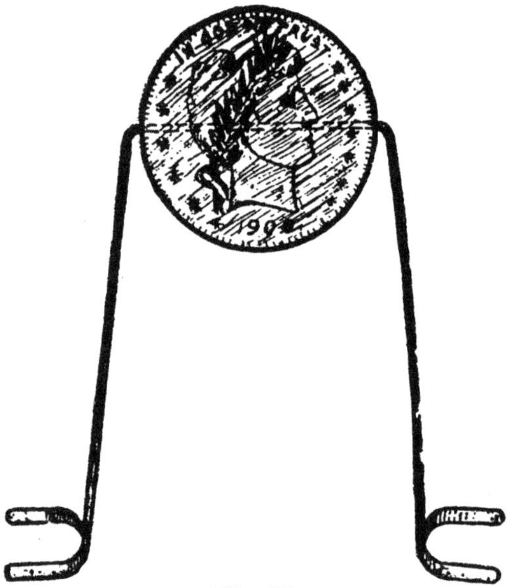

Fig. 72.

tached to which is a wire (B) running from edge to edge of the coin. When the apparatus is placed in proper position it will be found that the reverse palm can be easily executed.

The coin next to be described is the invention

of Mr. William J. Hilliar, and is an improvement on the foregoing, inasmuch as the fingers can be spread open. It consists of two thin coins, brazed together, through which runs a piece of fine elastic, which admits of great extension. The elastic terminates on either side of the coin in catgut loops, which fit over first and

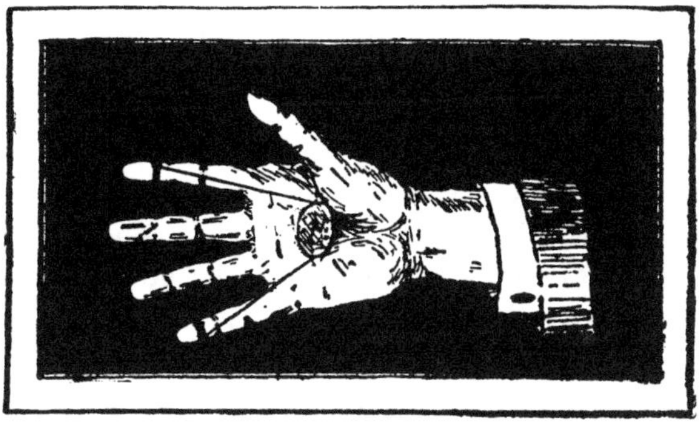

Fig. 73.

fourth fingers. The ordinary reverse palm can now be accomplished, but when it is desired to show nothing between the fingers, all that is necessary is to push down the coin with the two middle fingers into the palm which grips it tightly, the elastic, of course, stretching sufficiently to admit of this (*see Fig.* 73). When the back of the hand is shown to the audience the elastic is completely hidden by the first and fourth fingers. To show the front of the hand the coin is simply released from palm when it flies to finger tips, from whence it is transferred to the back of the hand.

NOTE—A new mechanical coin by the aid of which the continuous back and front palm has recently brought out by Mr. Roterberg, and is furnished by the publisher. The coin instead of being brazed together is a single one with a hole drilled clear through it. Through this is passed a wire, to either end of which are soldered tiny flesh-colored clips. This mechanical coin, which eclipses any other coin for the purpose described, can be used by anyone with ease and without the least fear of detection.

The author specially recommends this coin, as he considers it to be the best adaptation of the "Spider" idea that he is acquainted with.

Innumerable other mechanical coins, invented for the same purpose as the foregoing, are to be obtained from the publisher, of Chicago, and of other magical dealers. The author would recommend a purchaser to obtain two, or even three different coins, as he can then use the one that suits him best, some of the devices being far more suitable for one person's hand than another.

Either of the above mentioned coins can be used for imitating the author's feat of passing a coin through the knee, but in this case, of course, one must be attached to each hand.

A great number of "coin holders" are used in different ways by magicians, enabling them to deal easily with a large number of coins. The holder now about to be described is used for the purposes of getting the first stack of coins on to the rim of the hat, and subsequently into the hat for the purpose of dropping one at a time, the sleight-of-hand method of which is explained in Chapter II.

Fig. 74 shows the appearance of the holder which is constructed on the principle of the well-known sovereign purse, the top being attached to a spiral spring which can be depressed, but immediately resumes its original position. It is obvious, therefore, that if a coin is removed another one immediately takes its place. Soldered to the holder are two hooks to attach same to the lining of the hat, thereby enabling the performer to remove the left hand, if desired. In the opinion of the author the hooks are rather more bother than use, as, for instance, in the act of removing the holder from the pocket, the hooks are just as likely as not to catch in something. The holder should be painted a dead black, thus considerably minimizing the chances of its being observed.

While on the subject of hat "fakes" the author will now describe an exceedingly ingenious piece of apparatus, invented by Mr. M. M.

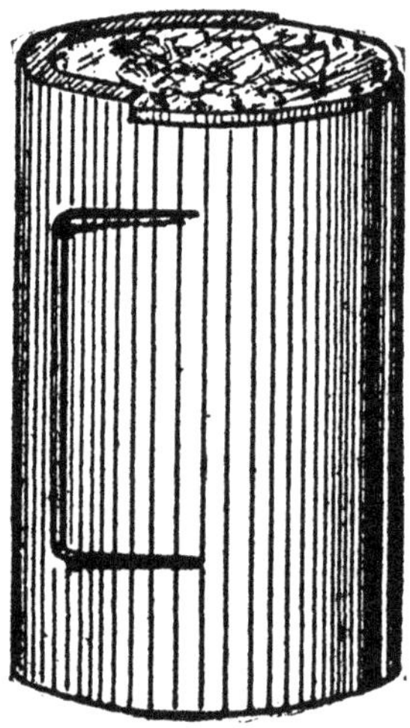

Fig. 74.

Wood, of Chicago. It is so constructed that, during the performance of "The Miser's Dream," the artist can at any moment (by making use of this apparatus) show both hands empty, and to alleviate any suspicion that the coins drop into the hat from the left hand, the hat can be held on the palm of the hand. Notwithstanding this, coins can be caught in the air with the right hand and thrown apparently into the hat, same being distinctly heard to fall. This can be repeated a number of times.

The piece of apparatus necessary for producing the above effect is that depicted in *Fig.* 75: A is a holder made of brass, the capacity of

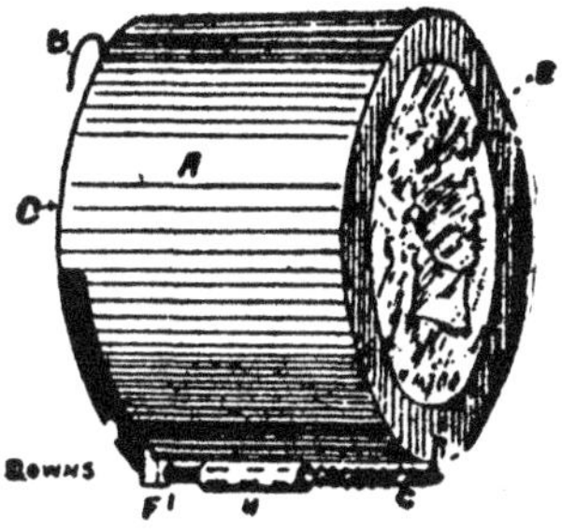

Fig. 75.

which is sufficient to hold easily six half-dollars. To the bottom plate (D) of same are fastened two tiny hooks (B) which enable the performer to suspend same wherever most get-at-able, for instance, behind coat tails; C is a slot extending in front of the bottom plate (D) to the middle of the holder. The slot is big enough to allow the insertion of one half-dollar at a time into the holder. Opposite to the bottom plate (D) is the bottom (E) of the holder, which is provided with a hole sufficiently large to admit the easy insertion of the tip of the middle finger. The first coin to drop rests in front of the slot (C), and to prevent it from dropping prematurely, a lever (H) is fixed below the holder, sideways to the slot (C). The lever is pushed forward and turned round so that the little metal clip (F) of same enters the slot (C). A spiral spring fixed to the lever (H) has the effect of drawing the lever back, so that as soon as the metal clip (F) enters the slot (C) it is held in position by the spring.

Provided with the above the performer goes hat in hand among the audience, allowing them to inspect the hat. While this is being done he indetectably obtains possession of the holder from wherever it was secreted, and as he returns to the stage he manages to fix it into the hat by hanging it on both hooks (B) to the leather rim. He now presses down the hook (G) of the lever (H), thereby opening the slot (C). To prevent the coin laying in front of the aperture (C) from falling out now the hat is slightly tilted, so that the coins rest on the bottom (E)

CPSIA information can be obtained
at www.ICGtesting.com
Printed in the USA
BVHW041052081119
563279BV00014B/1156/P

9 781163 145630